The
DICTIONARY
of POSH

The
DICTIONARY
P*of*OSH

Incorporating the Fall and Rise
of the Pails-Hurtingseaux Family

HUGH KELLETT

Illustrations by
OLIVER PRESTON

Quiller

Introduction to *The Dictionary of Posh: Incorporating the Fall and Rise of the Pails-Hurtingseaux Family*

E stuary English is a powerful thing. In a few short years it has pretty well managed to drive from our shores the old cut-glass enunciation of English so beloved of royalty, antique BBC presenters and 50's films stars.

The good news is that the old tongue is still there, just, hanging on.

The Dictionary of Posh: Incorporating the Fall and Rise of the Pails-Hurtingseaux Family serves as an essential guide to the (ab)use of many English words by the decidedly up-market, and the resultant – and endangered – language they speak: Posh.

Now you can learn Posh too (or polish it up if you're a native speaker) and be part of its preservation!

The book comes in the form of a dictionary, each word listed being genuine English and of familiar spelling to the average reader. But when translated into Posh these words take on very different meanings, often with side-splitting consequences, so learning Posh is really marvellous fun.

To assist the learner in rapid mastery of the language, and to ensure correct understanding and future usage, helpful examples of the various words in the dictionary are given in context, and students will be talking Posh in no TAME at all. Improvement in social standing and employment prospects will normally follow quite speedily.

These helpful examples are revealed through the dictionary in **The Fall and Rise of the Pails-Hurtingseaux Family**, the sorry saga of the lives of the extended family of Viscount Pails-Hurtingseaux, whose story of riches, ruin and redemption this book really is.

Thus, it may not be too lofty a premiss to claim that this volume constitutes a *lexiconic novel*; and it may equally safely be said, dear reader, that this particular genre has never before been attempted.

Acknowledgement

I am indebted to Keith Hancock of Falmouth for the initial stimulation for this tome and for his contribution of the word EARS, which, being translated into Posh, means 'yes'. Try it.

Copyright © Hugh Kellett (text) 2019
Copyright © Oliver Preston (illustrations) 2019

First published in the UK in 2019 by
Quiller, an imprint of Quiller Publishing Ltd

British Library Cataloguing-in-Publication Data
A catalogue record for this book is available from
the British Library

ISBN 978-1-84689-304-9

Designed by Guy Callaby
Printed in China

Quiller
An imprint of Quiller Publishing Ltd
Wykey House, Wykey, Shrewsbury SY4 1JA
Tel: 01939 261616 Fax: 01939 261606
E-mail: info@quillerbooks.com
Website: www.quillerpublishing.com

To
MAY WAIF

The Setting for the Fall and Rise of the Pails-Hurtingseaux Family

The Fall and Rise of the Pails-Hurtingseaux Family, the story that runs through this dictionary, is set mainly in Hurtingseaux Castle, a crumbly Norman keep, seat of the current Viscount, Lord Pails-Hurtingseaux. Other locations are the fashionable venues and seasonal watering holes of the well-heeled, mainly in London and the Home Counties.

The Main Cast

Lord Pails-Hurtingseaux	Viscount and owner of Hurtingseaux Castle
Lady Pails-Hurtingseaux	His lady wife

Rupert	
Priscilla	Their offspring

Mr Harry Flesh-Herries	Lady P-H's brother
Mrs Daphne Flesh-Herries	His wife

Godfrey	
Bunty	Their offspring

Archie MacSporranhead	A distant relative of Lord P-H
Spraint	Lord P-H's butler
Mrs Sloppetty	The cook
Snitcher	The tenant farmer, gamekeeper and odd job man
Poppy	Lady P-H's lady's maid
Inspector Moleskin	The local constabulary

Lord
Pails-Hurtingseaux

Lady
Pails-Hurtingseaux

Mr Harry
Flesh-Herries

Mrs Daphne
Flesh-Herries

Rupert

Priscilla

Godfrey

Bunty

Archie
MacSporranhead

Spraint

Mrs Sloppetty

Snitcher

Poppy

Inspector
Moleskin

The Dictionary of Posh: Incorporating the Fall and Rise of the Pails-Hurtingseaux Family

NOTE: to simplify learning, each word of Posh is introduced individually in alphabetical order; after its introduction it is then CAPITALISED and replaces the conventional English word in the ensuing pages, so familiarity with the language builds at a gradual pace, and by the end total fluency will be achieved.

The student reader is encouraged to find a private place and pronounce the words of Posh out loud, perhaps in front of a mirror. It is good form in this respect for gentlemen students to enunciate Posh with their mouths held as tightly shut as possible and talk, with a slightly pained look, through their teeth (*see* HRH Prince Charles for correct style and nuancing of diction). For ladies, a more open-mouthed braying technique is to be encouraged, which adds considerable tone and authenticity to the end result.

A

ACE: (Noun)
Meaning: The state attained by water at 0 degrees centigrade
Example: *The whole family had gathered in the great hall of Hurtingseaux Castle and Lady Pails-Hurtingseaux told Spraint the butler, and not for the first time, that she desired four cubes of ACE in her lunchtime G&T*

ACORN: (Noun)
Meaning: In technology, a graphic representation
Example: *Rupert, Lord Pails-Hurtingseaux's son and heir, had grappled for years with his new-fangled lap top but could not understand what this particular desktop ACORN meant*

ADA: (Noun)
Meaning: A sea bird whose plumage is much revered for its softness

Example: *Bunty, the daughter of Harry and Daphne Flesh-Herries, returned from hunting and jumped straight into her bed whose duvet was made of the finest ADA down*
(*See also* BARD, DARK, GRICE, ISLE, PALAVER, SNAPE, SWORN)

AERO*: (Noun)
Meaning: A projectile
Example: *Lord Pails-Hurtingseaux was asking himself what exactly was meant by the expression "slings and AEROS of outrageous fortune"*

AIDS: (Noun)
Meaning: A date in March unlucky for Julius Caesar
Example: *Rupert could remember his latin teacher batting on about the AIDS of March but had no idea at all what he meant*

---

* *The slightly Germanic pronunciation, for instance of Aero for Arrow in Posh, raises the intriguing possibility of what might be coined an aristocratic hangover from the Hanoverian reign, with English courtiers of that period perhaps mimicking the king's German umlauted ä. There is precedence for this: the ingratiating Spanish did something similar when aping the lisp of one of their earlier kings, and still do to this day when ordering a cerveza.*

AIL: (Noun)
Meaning 1: A piece of land surrounded by water
Example: *The whole family agreed that the only saving grace of the AIL of Wight was Cowes week*

Meaning 2: The walkway in the middle of a church
Example: *Lord P-H was sadly not convinced that Rupert would ever walk down the AIL*

AIL: (Verb)
Meaning: I will
Example: *"Well AIL be blowed!" said Lord P-H on hearing from Spraint that the stock market had got a little volatile*

AIM: (Verb)
Meaning: I exist
Example: *"AIM really feeling a little under the weather today," said Lady P-H to her maid Poppy*

AIR: (Exclamation)
Meaning: An expression of surprise or mild shock

Example: *"AIR!" exclaimed Priscilla , the P-H's daughter, on being told that Daphne F-H, her rather loud aunt (on her mother's side) had already been accepted as a member of the Royal Yacht Squadron*

AIR: (Noun)
Meaning: An organ
Example: *Harry F-H, Lady P-H's brother, thought it essential to always keep an AIR to the ground*

AIR MAIL: (Noun)
Meaning: A consumer loyalty award
Example: *Daphne F-H, Lady P-H's sister-in-law, said only very common people would ever think of actually using their AIR MAILS*

ALLIANCE: (Noun)
Meaning: A regular amount of money paid into one's bank
Example: *Not for the first time, Lord P-H was wondering if he could afford to continue paying Rupert's rather hefty monthly ALLIANCE*

A

ANY: (Proper noun, name)
Meaning: Girl's name as in Oakley

ARDOUR: (Noun)
Meaning: Part of a cow's milk producing apparatus
Example: *Rupert was saying that Snitcher (the tenant farmer) was rubbing a cow's ARDOUR in a most peculiar way* (**See also CAR, MEMORIES**)

ARE: (Noun)
Meaning: Sixty minutes

ARSE: (Pronoun)
Meaning: A reference to more than one person as the object of a verb or preposition
Example: *"Forgive ARSE our trespasses..."*

ARTILY: (Adverb)
Meaning: Totally
Example: *Lady P-H was ARTILY convinced that it was the influx of unwashed Europeans that had brought on her latest illness*

ASHLEY: (Adverb)
Meaning: In fact
Example: *Priscilla's fav film was Love ASHLEY*

AUDLEY: (Adverb)
Meaning: Strangely
Example: *Bunty was thinking that her cousin Rupert had begun to behave really rather AUDLEY whenever she turned up at Hurtingseaux in her body-hugging riding gear* (**See also ORDERLY**)

AUKS: (Noun)
Meaning: A large bovine creature
Example: *Rupert had asked Mrs Sloppetty the cook to prepare nice AUKS tongue sandwiches for next Saturday's shoot*

AVIARY: (Noun)
Meaning: Tusk material
Example: *Lord P-H had a world class display of AVIARY in the Great Hall of the castle*

AWFUL: (Noun)
Meaning: Edible animal innards

Example: *Priscilla watched Mrs Sloppetty who was busily picking over her weekly supply of AWFUL*

AWN: (Preposition)
Meaning: Above
Example: *Rupert was lying AWN his bed reading the Beano*

B

BABEL*: (Noun)
Meaning: A holy book
Example: *Lady P-H always set the dogs AWN those ghastly Jehovah's Witnesses and other BABEL bashers*

BAIL: (Noun)
Meaning: A black bodily fluid
Example: *Lady P-H put her sombre mood that day down to a problem with her BAIL duct*

BAIT: (Noun)
Meaning: A rapid meal
Example: *The whole party slipped out of the Chelsea Flower Show for a quick BAIT and a bottle of champers*

BAHT: (Noun)
Meaning: A posterior
Example: *Harry F-H had always much admired Poppy's BAHT (**See also** BALM, BOUGHT)*

BAIRN: (Verb)
Meaning: To outlaw
Example: *Lady P-H thought it would be best to BAIRN all foreigners, particularly if they couldn't speak English (**See also** BEN)*

BAKE: (Noun)
Meaning: A form of two-wheeled transport
Example: *Rupert had always*

* *The main phonetical characteristic of Posh is the transposition of one vowel sound for another (see Appendix). A particularly significant instance of this is in the substitution of 'i' for 'a' - for example Spice is pronounced Space in Posh. This produces the ultimate distinction in that it is exactly the inverse of Posh's arch enemy, the dreaded Cockney, wherein Space becomes Spice.*

fancied his cousin Bunty but acknowledged she might ASHLEY *be a bit of a BAKE*

BALM: (Noun)
Meaning: A posterior
Example: *Bunty was looking over her shoulder in the mirror and wondered if her new jodhpurs made her BALM look too big* (**See also BOUGHT**)

BARBEL: (Noun)
Meaning: A tiny pocket of air in a liquid
Example: *Bunty was always particularly frisky after a nice chilled bottle of BARBELS*

BARD: (Noun)
Meaning 1: A flying target
Example: *Lord P-H was asking Snitcher how many BARDS were being put down this year*
(**See also DARK, GRICE, ISLE, PALAVER, SNAPE, SWORN**)

Meaning 2: The early stage of a flower
Example: *Priscilla was in the garden sniffing the rose BARDS and writing a short poem to them*

BARED: (Noun)
Meaning: A sleeping place
Example: *It was midday and Rupert was thinking it was possibly time to get out of BARED* (**See also SEC**)

It was midday and Rupert was thinking it was possibly time to get out of BARED

BARELY: (Noun)
Meaning: An abdominal protrusion
Example: *Godfrey, Harry F-H's sporty son, was inspecting his figure in the mirror and grumbling to himself about the arrival of a detectable beer BARELY*

BARK: (Noun)
Meaning: Responsibility
Example: *Harry F-H was in absolutely no doubt that the BARK stopped with other people*

BARKER: (Noun)
Meaning: An item of headgear
Example: *Lady P-H abominated all foreigners, particularly Arabs, and especially those in BARKERS*

BARKS: (Proper noun, place name)
Meaning: A county north of London, home to High Wycombe and Milton Keynes. *Never to be confused with Berks*

BARN: (Noun)
Meaning: A small loaf (*See also* BEAGLE, BEGET, SCORN)

BARNEY: (Noun)
Meaning: A small animal with big AIRS
Example: *Priscilla just adored playing with her BARNEY (See also RAREBIT)*

BART: (Conjunction)
Meaning: Then again, alternatively
Example: *Bunty liked Moët BART loved Bolly, which had more BARBELS*

BARTER: (Noun)
Meaning: A spread made of churned cream
Example: *People always said that BARTER wouldn't melt in Poppy's mouth*

BARTON: (Noun)
Meaning: A fastening device
Example: *Rupert could never have been accused of having his finger AWN the BARTON (See also PAUPER)*

BARTOK: (Noun)
Meaning: Half of a BALM
Example: *Harry F-H accidentally brushed his hand against Poppy's left BARTOK*

BASIN: (Noun)
Meaning: A big shaggy bovine
Example: *Lord P-H had once nearly been shat AWN by a BASIN when visiting his cousin at Longleat*

BATH: (Noun)
Meaning: The process of coming into this world
Example: *Lord P-H was philosophical enough to recognise that his wealth was really all down to an accident of BATH*

BAUBLE: (Noun)
Meaning: A pompom
Example: *Priscilla's new grunge look involved her wearing a woolly hat with a BAUBLE AWN the top*

*Harry F-H accidentally brushed his hand against Poppy's left **BARTOK***

BAULKS: (Noun)
Meaning: A small container often made of wood
Example: *Daphne F-H's main objective in life was for just one invite to the Royal BAULKS*

BAWDY: (Noun)
Meaning: Silhouette
Example: *Rupert was lying in bed thinking about the delightful curves of cousin Bunty's perfect BAWDY*

BAY: (Verb)
Meaning 1: To purchase
Example: *Daphne F-H was absolutely firm in her conviction that money definitely could BAY happiness*

BAY: (Preposition)
Meaning 2: Via
Example: *BAY Royal Appointment*

BAYONET: (Proper noun, name)
Meaning: Surname of family in Pride and Prejudice
Example: *"Gordon BAYONET!" shouted Lord P-H AWN receiving a bill for £45,000 from his lady wife's doctor*

BEAGLE: (Noun)
Meaning: A BARN with a hole
Example: *Rupert was slowly toasting a BEAGLE AWN the Aga (**See also** BEGET, SCORN)*

BECALM: (Verb)
Meaning: To turn into
Example: *Lady P-H was rolling her eyes and bemoaning what the country had BECALM since the loss of Empire*

BECK: (Noun)
Meaning: A part of the BAWDY
Example: *Lady P-H was AWN route that day to Harley Street to see her doctor about her BECK*

BECKER: (Noun)
Meaning: A financial sponsor
Example: *When Godfrey had needed funding from the City in the past he had had no trouble finding a suitable BECKER*

BECKIE: (Noun)
Meaning: A smoking material
Example: *When rolling a joint*

B

Priscilla always made sure not to go too heavy AWN the BECKIE

BED: (Adjective)
Meaning: Immoral
Example: *Rupert thought it was probably BED to fancy his cousin Bunty BART he just couldn't help it* (**See also HOBBLE, TEARABLE**)

BEG: (Noun)
Meaning: A carrying device
Example: *Daphne F-H had just spent £2,500 AWN a new BEG for Cheltenham* (**See also SEC**)

BEGET: (Noun)
Meaning: An item in a boulangerie
Example: *Rupert had smuggled a BEGET into the castle despite his mama's BAIRN AWN foreign food, particularly French* (**See also SCORN**)

BELATED: (Verb, past tense)
Meaning: Spoilt
Example: *Lady P-H was complaining that those ghastly windfarms BELATED the landscape*

BELLY: (Noun)
Meaning: Dancing to music
Example: *If there was one part of the season Lord P-H could not abide it was the BELLY at Sadler's Wells*

BEN: (Verb) *See* **BAIRN**

BEND: (Noun)
Meaning: A group of musicians
Example: *Priscilla could hardly contain herself when she heard that her favourite BEND was playing at Glasto*

BEND: (Verb)
Meaning: Past tense of BEN

BENDY: (Adjective)
Meaning: Bowlegged
Example: *Bunty worried whether all this riding was making her legs BENDY. Or was it something else?*

BENGAL: (Noun)
Meaning: A personal ornament
Example: *Priscilla was in a hippy mood that morning and*

*Priscilla had a hangover and hadn't felt this BED since the **BERYL** of her first guinea pig*

wore a large BENGAL AWN each wrist

BERATE: (Adjective)
Meaning: Positive, cloudless
Example: *Daphne F-H always felt her husband's wealth guaranteed her a particularly BERATE future* (***See also** SARNIE*)

BERET: (Proper noun, name)
Meaning: As in Gibb

BERYL: (Noun)
Meaning 1: Interment
Example: *Priscilla had a hangover and hadn't felt this BED since the BERYL of her first guinea pig*

Meaning 2: A cask
Example: *Lord P-H would not admit this to anyone BART his trusted butler Spraint, BART it appeared his many creditors were beginning to get him over a BERYL*

Meaning 3: A part of a gun
Example: *In fact Lord P-H felt he might not just be over a BERYL BART also staring down one*

B

BETTER: (Noun)
Meaning: A mixture of flour and milk
Example: *Mrs Sloppetty was famous for the sogginess of her BETTER*

BETTING: (Noun)
Meaning: In, as in cricket

BETTY: (Adjective)
Meaning: Unhinged
Example: *Rupert was ASHLEY BECALMING ARTILY BETTY about Bunty* (**See also MED, MERDE**)

BHAJI: (Noun)
Meaning: A small BARD popular in council flats
Example: *Priscilla was absolutely mortified when her favourite BHAJI flew off into the wood and was never seen again*

BILE: (Noun)
Meaning: Intestine
Example: *Lady P-H was AWN the phone trying to convince her doctor that there was definitely something fishy going AWN with her large BILE*

BIND: (Noun)
Meaning: Leap
Example: *At lunch AWN Sunday Rupert made a slightly ungainly BIND and was at Bunty's side in one*

BINDER: (Noun)
Meaning: An untrustworthy or dishonourable male person
Example: *Harry F-H's chums at the golf club wouldn't ASHLEY call him a cad, BART acknowledged him certainly to be something of a BINDER*

BISLEY: (Adverb)
Meaning: Actively, with enthusiasm
Example: *Rupert was BISLEY thinking up as many ways as poss to get Bunty into the sack*

BITE: (Noun)
Meaning: A fight in a series
Example: *Lady P-H was moaning to Poppy that she was confined to her BARED with a BED BITE of flu that had almost certainly come from China or somewhere equally ghastly*

BLEND: (Adjective)
Meaning: Innocuous
Example: *The very best that could be said of Mrs Sloppetty's signature dish "coq au vin rusticana" was that it was pleasingly BLEND*

BLOW: (Adverb)
Meaning: Down there
Example: *Lady P-H was in the castle library reading up AWN all the medical problems one can get down BLOW*

BOARD: (Noun)
Meaning: A male
Example: *Harry F-H liked a day at Silverstone with the other BOARDS from the racing circuit (See also CHARM)*

BORG: (Noun)
Meaning: A WC
Example: *Spraint had respectfully placed a fresh copy of the Sun in Lord P-H's private BORG before breakfast (See also LEVY)*

BOROUGH: (Noun)
Meaning: A place AWN the farm where a BARNEY makes his home

BORN: (Adjective)
Meaning: Good in French, one of only two words that Rupert had learnt at school (See also JAW)

BORTSCH: (Noun)
Meaning: A mistake or cock up
Example: *Harry F-H was AWN the phone that morning to the Aston Martin dealer complaining of the BORTSCH job they had done AWN his rear bumper*

BOUGHT: (Noun)
Meaning: A posterior
Example: *Rupert had sat there fantasising for an ARE about Bunty's BOUGHT*

BRA: (Noun)
Meaning: A thicket
Example: *Snitcher had apparently complained that the hedgerow along the long field was so overgrown it had BECALM something of a BRA*

BRAID: (Noun)
Meaning: A female person getting married
Example: *Rupert was now*

*Lord P-H found that a large bowl of **BREN** each morning made his daily visit to his **BORG** more productive*

seriously wondering if he could make Bunty his BRAID and had snuck off to research the sex and incest thingy regarding first cousins

BRAINY: (Noun)
Meaning: Sea
Example: *The whole party was mortified when Daphne F-H drank so many bottles of BARBELS at Cowes she fell headfirst into the BRAINY*

BRANCH: (Noun)
Meaning: A late morning repast

Example: *Lady P-H excoriated the concept of BRANCH as an unnatural abomination, an invention of Americans or arrivistes probably from Essex*

BREAD: (Proper noun, name)
Meaning: As in Pitt

BREN: (Noun)
Meaning: A form of roughage
Example: *Lord P-H found that a large bowl of BREN each morning made his daily visit to his BORG more productive*

BRETT: (Noun)
Meaning: A small person
Example: *Lady P-H was intolerant of noisy children and had been known to incarcerate any offending BRETT in the cellar*

BRINE: (Adjective)
Meaning: Earth coloured

Example: *Priscilla wondered if Snitcher ever washed his hands as they were permanently BRINE*

BRIONY: (Noun)
Meaning: A small chocolatey cake
Example: *Bunty couldn't make up her mind if a BRIONY was ASHLEY better than sex*

*Bunty couldn't make up her mind if a **BRIONY** was ASHLEY better than sex*

The story so far ...

Unbeknownst to all but **Spraint, Lord P-H** is experiencing money problems on multiple fronts: the crippling bills that his hypochondriac wife is clocking up, his son **Rupert**'s allowance and, not least, the pending threat of a stock market crash that his Lordship has read about in The Sun. The farm itself also appears to be deteriorating. Away from all this gloom, life rolls by in glorious insouciance: **Rupert** is falling for his cousin **Bunty**, and **Harry Flesh-Herries** has got bedroom plans for **Poppy**. **Bunty** herself has no interest in **Rupert**, preferring to focus on the more serious stuff of fox hunting and chocolate, although she is getting concerned about the size of her bum. **Godfrey** is sailing close to the wind with his gambling, **Priscilla** is too stoned to know what day it is and **Mrs Sloppetty** is aiding the family's indigestion.

C

CABER: (Proper noun, place name)
Meaning: A pass between India and Pakistan where His Lordship had served with great distinction with the Royal Engineers

CAFFREY: (Adjective)
Meaning: Happy and unconcerned
Example: *Priscilla felt totally CAFFREY as she lit up, and plucked the petals from a darling little daisy*

CAIRN: (Verb)
Meaning: Present tense of to be able
Example: *Voicemail to Bunty: 'CAIRN I take you to the pictures? Love Rupert'* (**See also** KEN)

CALF: (Noun)
Meaning: End of a sleeve
Example: *Godfrey's Rolex peeped out from behind a beautifully starched CALF*

CALLER: (Noun)
Meaning: Top of a shirt
Example: *Godfrey's CALLER was of course as impeccable as his CALF*

CALM: (Verb)
Meaning: To travel or arrive
Example: *Dear Bunty: Please CALM to dinner. Love Rupert XXX*

CANED: (Noun)
Meaning: Type
Example: *Poppy was absolutely Harry F-H's CANED of girl*

CAR: (Noun)
Meaning: Bovine animal
Example: *Rupert was slightly alarmed that morning to see Snitcher with his left hand right up a CAR'S BALM (**See also** KETTLE)*

CARACAS: (Adjective)
Meaning: Bonkers
Example: *Harry F-H hated to admit the fact that he was going slightly CARACAS about Poppy*

CARD: (Noun)
Meaning: Partly digested grass inside a CAR
Example: *Snitcher was seen leaning AWN a fence*

scratching his BALM while the CARS were chewing the CARD and farting liberally

CARLA: (Noun)
Meaning: A hue
Example: *The only CARLA Lady P-H believed in was English White*

CARNAL: (Noun, title)
Meaning: An officer
Example: *When serving with great distinction with the Royal Engineers Lord P-H had attained the rank of Lieutenant-CARNAL*

CARP: (Noun)
Meaning: A drinking vessel
Example: *Rupert was complaining that Mrs Sloppetty couldn't even make a CARP of tea*

CART: (Verb)
Meaning: To chop
Example: *Harry F-H always reckoned he CART a fine figure in the Aston*

C

Harry F-H always reckoned he
CART *a fine figure in the Aston*

CARTONS: (Noun plural)
Meaning: Drapes
Example: *It was 9:30 am and
His Lordship was surprised that
Spraint had not yet opened the
CARTONS in the library*

CARVER: (Noun)
Meaning: Protection
Example: *Lord P-H asked
Rupert to make sure that the*
*insurance CARVER AWN the
castle was up to date...and Rupert
simply added another zero to its
insured value*

CASTER: (Proper noun, name)
**Meaning: As in General,
7th Cavalry, Lord P-H's hero**

CAULI: (Noun)
Meaning: A sheep dog

CAULKER: (Noun)
Meaning: A type of spaniel, plentiful at Hurtingseaux

CEILIDH: (Proper noun, name)
Meaning: Inferior class name, as in Minogue

CELERY: (Noun)
Meaning: Income
Example: *Lord P-H confessed he was ill-equipped to offer advice to Rupert AWN what to expect in a CELERY as he himself hadn't recently had one*

CENTRE: (Proper noun, name)
Meaning: Who Lord P-H dresses up as at Christmas

CEP: (Noun)
Meaning: A plant fluid
Example: *Whenever Harry F-H saw Poppy he felt the CEP was definitely rising*

CHABLIS: (Adverb)
Meaning: Untidy
Example: *All concurred that it was impossible to be more*

CHABLIS attired than Snitcher (**See also** HAWK, MERLOT, TRAIN)

CHAIRS: (Exclamation)
Meaning: All the best, chin-chin, bottoms up, down the hatch

CHALKY: (Noun)
Meaning; A piece of confectionery
Example: *Bunty had received a BAULKS of Milk Tray from Rupert and she was wondering which CHALKY to have first*

CHARM: (Noun)
Meaning: A friend
Example: *Despite the BAULKS of CHALKS, Bunty was keen to distance herself from Rupert and just remain CHARMS, BART then again it had to be admitted her BECALMING a chatelaine was quite an attractive proposition*

CHEVY: (Adjective)
Meaning: Of vulgar brash breeding
Example: *Godfrey was horrified that tattoos were creeping into the*

upper classes and saw them as
ARTILY CHEVVY

CHORD: (Noun)
Meaning: A fish
Example: *To raised eyebrows
Mrs Sloppetty was explaining
at dinner that the green looking
fish was CHORD, fresh that
very morning*

CLAIM: (Verb)
Meaning: To ascend
Example: *When serving with
great distinction with the Royal
Engineers, Lord P-H had
unsuccessfully attempted to
CLAIM Everest*

CLAIRE: (Adjective)
Meaning: Lucid
Example: *Daphne F-H made it
totally CLAIRE to her husband
that her pekingese should not
have to mix with his Lordship's
nasty randy CAULKER spaniels*

CLAWED: (Noun)
Meaning: A lump of earth
Example: *Snitcher could not go
anywhere without leaving a
tell-tale CLAWED behind him*

CLEANSE: (Noun, plural)
Meaning: Scottish family group
Example: *In the pamphlet he
had written AWN the family
history His Lordship had said
that his detested cousin Archie
MacSporranhead was a member
of one of the extremely inferior
CLEANSE*

CLEARANCE: (Proper noun,
name)
Example: *Lady P-H had once
had the pleasure of dining with
the late HRH The Queen Mother
in CLEARANCE House, and
found she agreed with her AWN
most things*

CLEMENT: (Noun)
**Meaning: Someone appealing
for something**
Example: *Her Ladyship was
protesting about a particular
benefit CLEMENT, and
complaining about those awful
scroungers from the EU and the
rest of the world generally*

CLEMMY: (Adjective)
**Meaning: Damp and sticky
often through fear**

Example: *The mere thought of Bunty in the buff made Rupert's hands go strangely CLEMMY*

CLERK: (Noun)
Meaning: The sound a chicken makes

CLONE: (Proper noun, place name)
Meaning: Germany city noted for its eau

CLOSE: (Noun plural)
Meaning: Apparel
Example: *Daphne F-H was of the opinion that one simply couldn't have too many CLOSE in one's wardrobe*

CLYDE: (Noun)
Meaning: A floaty thing
Example: *Priscilla had just shot up and there was suddenly not a CLYDE in the sky*

CORBEL: (Verb)
Meaning: To roughly improvise
Example: *Harry F-H was asking about the possibility of a 500 BARD day at Hurtingseaux for him and his CHARMS and Rupert said that he and his papa could probably CORBEL something together*

Lady P-H would let out a loud disapproving CORFE whenever a political subject with which she disagreed was raised at dinner

CORFE: (Noun)
Meaning: The noisy expulsion of air from the lungs
Example: *Lady P-H would let out a loud disapproving CORFE whenever a political subject with which she disagreed was raised at dinner*

CORK: (Noun)
Meaning (amongst others): A male game BARD
Example: *Lord P-H was asking Snitcher how many CORKS had made it through the winter*

CORN: (Verb)
Meaning: To swindle
Example: *Lord P-H was BECALMING concerned over his investments and whether someone was trying to CORN him, so he decided to talk to his old policeman friend, Inspector Moleskin, AWN the matter*

CORNY: (Proper noun, name)
Meaning: Girl's name as in Booth

CORPSE: (Noun)
Meaning 1: Constabulary, as in Inspector Moleskin's employer

Meaning 2: A wood
Example: *Snitcher was showing Rupert the pheasants in the CORPSE, BART Rupert couldn't help feeling there were far fewer BARDS than last season*

CORRECT: (Verb, past tense)
Meaning: Solved
Example: *Lord P-H was quietly pleased that he had finally CORRECT the last clue in The Sun crossword*

COURSE: (Proper noun, place name)
Meaning: An AIL off Greece

COURT: (Noun)
Meaning: A cradle
Example: *The 500 year old Pails-Hurtingseaux family COURT occupied a position AWN show at the top of the main staircase*

COWRY: (Noun)
Meaning: An Indian meal
Example: *Godfrey liked nothing better than a fiendishly hot COWRY with his BECKERS in the City*

CRAFTS: (Proper noun, name)
Meaning: A canine talent show
Example: *Bunty could think of nothing so ghastly and vulgar as CRAFTS, BART her Mama Daphne was ASHLEY thinking of entering her favourite Pekingese*

CRECHE: (Noun)
Meaning: A collapse
Example: *Lord P-H nearly had a heart attack when he read the shocking news of the stock market CRECHE in The Sun while astride his BORG*

CRÈME: (Verb)
Meaning: To stuff
Example: *Bunty wanted to CRÈME as many days hunting into her calendar as poss*

CREPE: (Noun)
Meaning: An activity in the BORG

CREPES: (Exclamation)
Meaning: Goodness me
Example: *CREPES! Yelled Lord P-H when he read about the stock market CRECHE AWN the BORG*

CREPT: (Verb)
Meaning: To have visited the BORG
Example: *Harry F-H was almost inconsolable at breakfast AWN discovering that a BARD had CREPT AWN the Aston*

CRESS: (Adjective)
Meaning: Stupid
Example: *At Eton, Rupert had always excelled at exhibiting CRESS stupidity*

CRIED: (Noun)
Meaning: A lot of people
Example: *Two's company...*

CROQUET: (Adjective)
Meaning: Hoarse
Example: *Lady P-H had no idea what was wrong BART she had woken up with a CROQUET voice and was reaching for the doctor's number*

CULT: (Noun, local dialect)
Meaning: A piece of Scottish attire
Example: *Lord P-H had also written in the family history that* *his detested cousin Archie McSporranhead was so stingy it was no surprise that he wore nothing under his CULT*

D

D

DACE: (Noun, plural)
Meaning: Gaming cubes
Example: *Following the terrible news of the CRECHE, and the decimation of his fortune, Lord P-H was wondering what the next roll of the DACE would bring him*

DAHL: (Verb)
Meaning: To select numbers on a telephone
Example: *Lady P-H was feeling so veritably indisposed that day she had had to ask Poppy if she could kindly DAHL the doctor for her*

DAME: (Noun)
Meaning: A small piece of currency
Example: *Lord P-H was shocked* *to read that some very rich Americans had been left without a DAME in previous CRECHES*

DANE: (Verb)
Meaning: To eat
Example: *Bunty was proclaiming with her mouth full that the lower classes eat BART the upper classes DANE*

DARK: (Noun)
Meaning: A swimming BARD
Example: *Godfrey was appalled when the England opener was out for a DARK at Lords*
(**See also GRICE, ISLE, PALAVER, SNAPE, SWORN**)

DARN: (Verb, past tense)
Meaning: Performed
Example: *Rupert had to admit*

Bunty was proclaiming with her mouth full that the lower classes eat BART the upper classes DANE

that he could not be described as having DARN well at anything

DART: (Noun)
Meaning: A food regime
Example: *Bunty was having trouble getting into her jodhpurs, despite their stretchiness, and decided there and then to go AWN an immediate DART*

DAVE: (Noun)
Meaning: A seedy place
Example: *Godfrey thought the Ritz had BECALM really a bit of a DAVE*

DAWDLE: (Noun)
Meaning: Something of ease

or simplicity
Example: *Godfrey had considered winning at poker an absolute DAWDLE until he lost fifty grand that evening after Lords*

DAWN: (Verb)
Meaning: To put AWN
Example: *Daphne F-H had decided to DAWN a feather boa for the garden fete*

DAY: (Verb)
Meaning: To expire
Example: *Lady P-H was always ARTILY certain she was about to DAY*

DEAD: (Noun)
Meaning: Father
Example: *Lord P-H insisted AWN being addressed as Father and disliked intensely being called DEAD BAY his children*

DEAF: (Noun)
Meaning: A spring flower
Example: *Priscilla was wandering barefoot in the orchard and bent down to smell a solitary DEAF*

DEB: (Noun)
Meaning: To blot
Example: *When Lord P-H realised the full scale of his losses he had to DEB his eye with a silk hankie that the simpering Spraint had kindly offered him*

DELI: (Verb)
Meaning: To hang about
Example: *Her Ladyship was urging Snitcher to look lively and not to dilly DELI so*

DEPRAVED: (Adjective)
Meaning: Lacking in everyday amenities

Example: *Bunty had heard the expression "DEPRAVED families" and thought they should probably be locked up for not trying hard enough*

DIGHT: (Noun)
Meaning: Suspicion
Example: *Harry F-H had no DIGHT that Poppy would CALM round to his way of thinking eventually*

DINE: (Preposition)
Meaning: Below
Example: *Apart from the Queen there was no-one Lady P-H didn't look DINE AWN*

DINING: (Adjectival place name)
Meaning: As in the street where the British PM lives

DORK: (Noun)
Meaning: A medical practitioner as in Holiday, Martin etc

DORM: (Monk's title)
Meaning: As in Perignon

D

DOWRY: (Noun)
Meaning: A book with days in it

DRAMA: (Noun)
Meaning: A percussionist
Example: *Priscilla was BETTY about the new DRAMA in her favourite BEND*

DRAY: (Adjective)
Meaning: Not wet

Example: *Spraint had advised his Lordship, albeit with a show of great reluctance, that the collection of DRAY Burgundies could fetch a decent price at auction*

DREG: (Noun)
Meaning: A draw
Example: *Priscilla took a long deep luxuriant DREG AWN her freshly rolled spliff*

*Priscilla was BETTY about the new **DRAMA** in her favourite BEND*

The story so far ...

The financial storm clouds gather and the loyalty of **Spraint** and **Snitcher** becomes ambiguous. **Rupert** and **Harry** maintain their sexual bids. **Rupert** has been tasked with renewing the castle's insurance cover and this he does by simply adding a nought to the previous year's sum. We learn of a detested Scottish relative, **Archie MacSporranhead**, whom **Lord P-H** has defamed in a family journal; and of his Lordship's distinguished service in the Royal Engineers. **Godfrey** keeps rolling the dice and **Lady P-H**'s hypochondria and love for her fellow man both worsen. Large shoot days for the coming season are organised, even if **Rupert** has noticed that stocks seem oddly low. **Daphne F-H** complains that the P-H dogs are interfering with her Pekingese. Then the stock market does indeed nose-dive and **Lord P-H** is cleaned out, a disaster that he prefers to share only with **Spraint**.

E

EARS: (Interjection)
Meaning: Affirmative
Example: *Q: What is the opposite of no? A: EARS*

EBBS: (Noun, plural)
Meaning: Stomach muscles
Example: *Rupert thought he was a pound or two overweight and should tone up his EBBS*

EDITION: (Noun)
Meaning: Arithmetic
Example: *Rupert had failed to grasp even the basics of EDITION* (**See also METHS**)

EFFLUENT: (Adjective)
Meaning: Rich
Example: *Daphne F-H reflected daily about how glorious it all was to be so wonderfully EFFLUENT*

EH: (Noun)
Meaning: An organ in the head out of which one sees

EH: (Pronoun)
Meaning: First person singular
Example: *"EH think therefore EH am," always struck Rupert as a dashed odd thing to say*

ELBA: (Noun)
Meaning: A part of the BAWDY that Rupert finds indistinguishable from his arse

ELEGY: (Noun)
Meaning: An adverse reaction to
Example: *Lady P-H was sure that Mrs Sloppetty's prune and burdock cordial had resulted in an unsightly ELEGY appearing in a private area of her BAWDY* (**See also ELEMENT, MELODY**)

ELEMENT: (Noun)
Meaning: An illness
Example: *Not a day went BAY without Lady P-H discovering some new and more ghastly ELEMENT* (**See also MELODY**)

ELEMENTARY: (Adjective)
Meaning: To do with internal plumbing
Example: *Lady P-H was explaining patiently to the DORK that it was ASHLEY nothing to do with her BAIL duct after all BART everything to do with her ELEMENTARY canal* (**See also QUENELLE**)

ELF: (Proper noun, name)
Meaning: Chippy working class name as in Garnett and Ramsay

ELLIE: (Proper noun, name)
Meaning: As in the boxer formerly known as Cassius Clay

EMBER: (Adjective)
Meaning: Orangey coloured
Example: *Harry F-H admitted to Inspector Moleskin that he had driven through the lights at 85 BART insisted that they had been AWN EMBER*

END: (Conjunction)
Meaning: With
Example: *Gin END tonic*

ENGELS: (Noun, plural)
Meaning: The degrees between various lines
Example: *Rupert had been a complete flop when it came to calculating the sum of the ENGELS in a triangle*

ENTRY: (Proper noun, place name)
Meaning: A northern racecourse

Example: *Godfrey would never normally travel north BART made an exception for ENTRY AWN Grand National day, where he ended up losing twenty grand*

ERASE: (Verb)
Meaning: To CALM up
Example: *Harry F-H's recurring dream was of the Queen knighting him END hearing the immortal words: "ERASE Sir Harry"*

ESCORT: (Proper noun, place name)
Meaning: A place in Berkshire
Example: *Bunty was extremely damning of the level of obvious riff raff in the Royal Enclosure at ESCORT this year*

ESTHER: (Noun)
Meaning: A pretty flower in the daisy family

Harry F-H's recurring dream was of the Queen knighting him END hearing the immortal words: "ERASE Sir Harry"

EX: (Noun)
Meaning: A cutting implement
Example: *Rupert was explaining that Snitcher needed his EX sharpened if he were to CART DINE the offending BRA*

EXCEL: (Noun)
Meaning: A part of a vehicle with wheels AWN
Example: *Harry F-H drove over a rut AWN the way to Glyndebourne END feared he might have damaged his rear EXCEL*

EXCESS: (Noun)
Meaning: Admission

Example: *Lady P-H thought that the tradesmen's EXCESS to the castle needed to be made CLAIRE to prevent a string of awful people CALMING to the main gate*

EXCISE: (Noun)
Meaning: A healthful activity
Example: *The only EXCISE Harry F-H wanted to take was AWN board Poppy*

EXPENSIVE: (Adjective)
Meaning: Wide
Example: *From the top of the castle's battlements one could enjoy EXPENSIVE views of the whole Hurtingseaux estate*

F

FABER: (Noun)
Meaning: A thread
Example: *Lord P-H loved Hurtingseaux with every FABER in his BAWDY*

FAILED: (Verb, past tense)
Meaning: To have placed on record

Example: *It was CLAIRE His Lordship had lost all his capital in the CRECHE END it was with heavy heart that he asked Spraint to find out how exactly one FAILED for bankruptcy*

FAINLY: (Adverb)
Meaning: At last

Example: *Godfrey was at the casino END was convinced his luck was FAINLY about to change*

FAIRY: (Noun)
Meaning: A passenger boat
Example: *Everyone at Cowes was complaining of the wash made BAY the ghastly FAIRY from Portsmouth*

FAR: (Verb)
Meaning: To discharge
Example: *Lord P-H's only after-dinner joke was that FAR would be the last word you'd hear if you were unlucky enough to be shot at dawn*

FARCE: (Noun)
Meaning: A to-do
Example: *Lady P-H was telling Poppy that her doctor had impertinently suggested she might be making a bit of a FARCE about nothing*

FARCI: (Adjective)
Meaning: Fastidious, exhibiting a FARCE
Example: *It would be an understatement to suggest that Lady P-H was a tad FARCI about her health*

FARMER: (Adjective)
Meaning: Less floppy
Example: *Bunty had started her DART BART was not sure her BALM was looking that much FARMER*

Bunty had started her DART BART was not sure her BALM was looking that much FARMER

FAST: (Adjective)
Meaning: Initial
Example: *Rupert was their FAST child, END Lord P-H had wondered privately after that why anyone would want another*

FATE: (Noun)
Meaning: A battle
Example: *Godfrey loved boxing END was looking forward to the big FATE*

FAV: (Noun)
Meaning: The number after four

FAVOUR: (Noun)
Meaning: A currency note
Example: *His Lordship had often remarked that Archie MacSporranhead's grip AWN a FAVOUR was more vice-like than all others in Scotland (**See also** PINED)*

FAWLEY: (Noun)
Meaning: Lack of good sense
Example: *Lord P-H had decided that it would be FAWLEY to try END explain the family's new straightened circumstances to Her Ladyship, END decided to keep his trap shut*

FEB: (Adjective)
Meaning: Good
Example: *"Howd'ya like my FEB new hat?" asked Daphne F-H loudly AWN entering the Royal Enclosure (**See also** GOURD)*

His Lordship had often remarked that Archie MacSporranhead's grip AWN a FAVOUR was more vice-like than all others in Scotland

FED: (Noun)
Meaning: A phase
Example: *Lord P-H had always assumed that Priscilla's drug taking was just a passing FED*

FEIGN: (Adjective)
Meaning: Fair
Example: *The weather looked set FEIGN for a week of racing*

FEIGNED: (Verb)
Meaning: To discover
Example: *It had BECALM increasingly difficult for Godfrey to FEIGNED a winner at the Royal meeting END he was losing big time*

FELLOW: (Adjective)
Meaning: Unused
Example: *For some reason Snitcher had advised his Lordship to leave about 50 acres FELLOW*

FEN: (Noun)
Meaning: An admirer
Example: *Priscilla was a great FEN of Glyndebourne as well as Glasto*

FETA: (Adjective)
Meaning: More corpulent
Example: *When strolling home after the Chelsea Flower Show Godfrey END Bunty were in total agreement that the lower classes did indeed seem to be getting FETA and FETA*

FETISH: (Adjective)
Meaning: Somewhat corpulent
Example: *Rupert said that Snitcher had told him that the bullocks were FETISH... BART he felt they should be FETA*

FILE: (Verb)
Meaning: To make dirty
Example: *Much to the family's utter chagrin, Daphne F-H's Pekingese had been caught AWN TV as it squatted to FILE the arena at CRAFTS*

FINDER: (Verb)
Meaning: To BECALM wrecked
Example: *Lord P-H was saying to Spraint that the family had existed for 500 years END had never experienced what it meant*

F

to FINDER, to which Sprint
nodded sympathetically

FINED: (Verb)
Meaning: Discovered
Example: *Lady P-H had
FINED a small weeping mole
in an embarrassing place*

FLAY: (Noun)
**Meaning: An unwholesome
insect**
Example: *Rupert was dreaming
of being a FLAY AWN the wall
in Bunty's bedroom*

FLESH: (Noun)
Meaning: A quick movement
Example: *Archie
MacSporranhead saw a 10p piece
AWN the pavement in Aberdeen
END was DINE AWN it in
a FLESH*

FLEX: (Noun)
Meaning: A type of crop
Example: *Lord P-H had
suggested to Snitcher that as the
returns from the milking herd
seemed so low they might try a
bit of FLEX next year*

FLIER: (Noun)
**Meaning: A naturally
occurring love token**
Example: *Rupert had decided
to sweeten up Bunty BAY
BAYING her a lovely bunch
of FLIERS*

FLIP: (Proper noun, name)
Example: *Lord P-H had never
quite understood what HM the
Queen had seen in FLIP*

FLIPS: (Proper noun, name)
**Meaning: A London auction
house**
Example: *Sprint had suggested
quietly to his Lordship that, to
pay his debts, he might care to
consult with his contact at Mssrs
FLIPS about the valuation of the
castle's art collection*

FOETAL: (Adjective)
Meaning: Deadly
Example: *Lady P-H was trying
to convince the nurse that her
latest ELEMENT would prove
FOETAL unless treated
immediately*

FORD: (Adjective)
Meaning: In front of you
Example: *The Pails-Hurtingseaux motto, when translated from the original latin, meant roughly "Best foot FORD"*

FOREPLAY: (Noun)
Meaning: Type of wood

FORKS: (Noun)
Meaning: A wild canine creature
Example: *Bunty was just born for FORKS hunting* (**See also JEKYLL**)

FRAY: (Verb)
Meaning: A method of cooking
Example: *In a moment of rare lucidity, not to say bravery, Priscilla asked Mrs Sloppetty to boil tongue in future not FRAY it*

FREIGHT: (Noun)
Meaning: A scare
Example: *To add to his woes Lord P-H got the FREIGHT of his life when news came through of a hurricane, END that there was therefore now a new problem for him at Lloyds of London*

G

GARGLE: (Noun)
Meaning: A grotesque architectural figure
Example: *Some years previously Lord P-H had had a GARGLE made in the very image of his detested Scottish relative Archie MacSporranhead*

GARTER: (Noun)
Meaning: A drainage device
Example: *Snitcher had been sent up a ladder to inspect the very BED state of the castle's GARTERS*

GAZE: (Noun, plural)
Meaning: Men
Example: *Daphne F-H always measured her GAZE BAY the size of their bank balances*

GEM: (Noun)
Meaning: A sweet spread
Example: *Rupert simply loved a*

*hot BEGET or currant BARN
with blackcurrant GEM*

GENTLE: (Adjective)
**Meaning: To do with DINE
there**
Example: *Lady P-H was
pretty sure she had some sort of
GENTLE infection, brought
AWN perhaps BAY lack of use*

GETTING: (Proper noun,
name)
**Meaning: As in Mike, English
cricketer, one of Godfrey's
old heroes**

GHANA: (Noun)
**Meaning: A member of the
Royal Artillery**
Example: *Although Lord P-H
had been in the Royal Engineers,
he would have been perfectly
FEIGN as a GHANA*

GHETTO: (Noun)
Meaning: A creamy cake
Example: *At the village summer
fete that year, Rupert bought
Bunty an enormous piece of
Black Forest GHETTO*

GLADE: (Verb)
Meaning: To move gracefully
Example: *Priscilla had just
finished a spectacular joint END
had begun to GLADE sweetly
across the lawn*

GLENS: (Noun, plural)
Meaning: Hormone producers
Example: *In the mirror that
morning Lady P-H saw she had a
BED case of swollen GLENS*

GNARL: (Adjective)
Meaning: No longer existing
Example: *Godfrey was seeking a
way to make his gambling debts
GNARL END void*

GNAWED: (Noun)
**Meaning: To indicate approval
with the head**
Example: *Spraint had informed
his Lordship of the value of his
ancestral paintings END the
latter had given a reluctant
GNAWED for them to be
auctioned off at FLIPS*

GORBALS: (Verb)
**Meaning: To eat in a hurry
with accompanying sounds**

Example: *Daphne F-H was saying that the only person who seemed partial to Mrs Sloppetty's "cuisine" was Snitcher "who GORBALS it up as soon as it's laid before him"*

GORED: (Noun)
Meaning: A deity
Example: *"My GORED, we're DARN for!" exclaimed Lady P-H when she heard about the sale of the art heirlooms over breakfast*

GORSE: (Noun)
Meaning: Whispers END rumours
Example: *Bunty literally couldn't survive without the monthly GORSE in Tatler*

GOURD: (Adjective)
Meaning: Morally upright
Example: *Priscilla used to be such a GOURD little girl before she took up with all those beastly druggies*

GRACE: (Proper noun, place name)
Meaning: Place between Albania END Turkey

GRAPE: (Verb)
Meaning: To complain
Example: *Lord P-H had invited Inspector Moleskin over to GRAPE to him about his financial problems END asked him to keep an EH AWN Spraint END possibly Snitcher, both of whom he felt were up to something fishy*

GRAPH: (Adjective)
Meaning: Brusque
Example: *Because of his ever mounting problems Lord P-H had BECALM somewhat GRAPH*

GREVILLE: (Noun)
Meaning: Small stones
Example: *Harry F-H was always careful when approaching Lord P-H's castle as the GREVILLE tended to damage the paintwork AWN the Aston*

GRICE: (Noun)
Meaning: A game BARD
Example: *Rupert had missed several GRICE in a row END was wondering if his BERYLS were quite straight (**See also** ISLE, PALAVER, SNAPE, SWORN)*

G

GRIND: (Noun)
Meaning: Arena
Example: *Godfrey never cared for the Fifth Test at the Oval, a nasty little GRIND unfashionably south of the river*

GUESS: (Noun)
Meaning: A fuel
Example: *Bunty was saying how Mrs Sloppetty had nearly blown up the castle the previous Christmas BAY leaving the GUESS AWN all night*

GYTE: (Noun)
Meaning: A disease often associated with overindulgence
Example: *Lady P-H's toes were hurting a little END she immediately diagnosed GYTE*

H

HADES: (Plural of proper noun, name)
Meaning: As in there are a lot of HADES in Germany END Austria

HAIR: (Adverb)
Meaning: Present
Example: *"CALM HAIR!" yelled Rupert at the new CAULKER, who did no such thing*

HAIRY: (Proper noun, name)
Meaning: As in Houdini, Redknapp, Flesh-Herries, Prince etc

HAITI: (Noun)
Meaning: A type of hybrid meal taken early evening, usually with poached eggs AWN toast, as well as BARNS with GEM END BARTER

HAKE: (Noun)
Meaning: A long walk
Example: *Daphne F-H was complaining that it was impossible to FEIGNED a taxi after the Chelsea FLIER Show END that she had had to HAKE the 500 yards all the way to Sloane Square*

*Daphne F-H was complaining that it was impossible to FEIGNED a taxi after the Chelsea FLIER Show END that she had had to **HAKE** the 500 yards all the way to Sloane Square*

HALF: (Noun)
Meaning: A mildly BED mood
Example: *To say that his Lordship was in a bit of a HALF about his precarious financial position was the ultimate understatement*

HARD: (Proper noun, name)
Meaning: As in Hughes, of Effingham etc (*See also* HIRED)

HARD: (Verb, past tense)
Meaning: To have given employment to
Example: *Daphne F-H was saying to HAIRY that it was time they HARD a permanent chauffeur*

HARMING: (Verb)
Meaning: A nasally noise
Example: *Priscilla was lying stoned in the orchard that was pleasantly HARMING with bumblebees*

HARNESS: (Noun)
Meaning: Title of monarch
Example: *HAIRY F-H was not quite sure if he would have to address The Queen as Your Majesty or Your Royal HARNESS*

HARP: (Verb, imperative)
Meaning: Command given to a dog to jump up AWN to a seat
Example: *Rupert was unsuccessfully urging the new CAULKER to HARP into the Landrover*

HARPIES: (Noun)
Meaning: A virulent venereal disease to be avoided at all costs
Example: *Lady P-H was trying to convince her gynaecologist that she had a BED case of GENTLE HARPIES BART could not imagine how she had CALM BAY it*

HATE: (Noun)
Meaning: Stature
Example: *Godfrey was above average HATE END looked DINE AWN those who were BLOW it*

HAUGHTY: (Noun)
Meaning: A rubber container to warm the BARED
Example: *Mrs Sloppetty still made Rupert a HAUGHTY each evening in winter*

HAULS: (Noun)
Meaning: Vacation
Example: *With no money left Lord P-H was not sure what they were going to do about HAULS that year*

HAWK: (Noun)
Meaning: German wine
Example: *While clearing out the cellar for the auction sale Spraint unearthed a few cases of long forgotten HAWK which he secretly sold to his CHARMS* (*See also* **MERLOT, TRAIN**)

HAY: (Adjective)
Meaning: Spaced out
Example: *Priscilla was trying to go a day without getting HAY*

HAYLEY: (Adverb)
Meaning: Extremely
Example: *Daphne F-H had been HAYLEY critical of the new dress code at ESCORT*

HEAD: (Verb)
Meaning: Past tense of have

HEART: (Noun)
Meaning: A shed-like structure

Example: *Lord P-H HEAD heard from Moleskin that Snitcher END Sprint seemed to be spending a lot of time in the keeper's HEART, possibly plotting something against his Lordships's interests* (***See also SHARED***)

HECK: (Noun)
Meaning: A ride
Example: *Bunty was up with the larks for a HECK on her favourite hunter*

HEISS: (Noun, Germanic derivation)
Meaning: A building where people live
Example: *Daphne F-H was always AWN the look-out for an even bigger HEISS in Chelsea*

HEM: (Noun)
Meaning: Part of a deceased pig
Example: *It was generally acknowledged that Mrs Sloppetty's HEM was all BART inedible END was normally best fed to the nearest CAULKER*

HENNA: (Proper noun, name)
Meaning: As in Lord P-H's favourite actress HENNA Gordon

HERALD: (Proper noun, name)
Meaning: As in Godwinson, McMillan, Pinter, Wilson

HEROD: (Proper noun, name)
Meaning: Founder of a Knightsbridge store END the place Daphne F-H is at her most content

HEROINE: (Adjective)
Meaning: Not GOURD
Example: *Godfrey couldn't deny that losing so much at gambling HEAD been a distinctly HEROINE experience... BART he would live to FATE another day*

HERRING: (Noun)
Meaning: Audio faculty
Example: *Lady P-H was increasingly concerned that she was slowly losing her HERRING*

HENS: (Noun)
Meaning: Things at the end of one's arms

Example: *HAIRY F-H couldn't wait to get his HENS AWN Poppy's delightful BOUGHT*

HET: (Noun)
Meaning: A piece of headgear
Example: *Daphne F-H HEAD worn a silk HET with a FAV foot wingspan to the garden party*

HIGH: (Adverb)
Meaning: In what way
Example: *"HIGH are you feeling today, Your Ladyship?" enquired her DORK with an air of resignation*

HIND: (Noun, plural HEINZ)
Meaning: A dog, particularly one that follows a FORKS

HOBBLE: (Adjective)
Meaning: BED, nasty
Example: *Bunty said that it was totally HOBBLE of the government to BEN FORKS hunting (**See also** TEARABLE)*

HOURLY: (Adverb)
Meaning: Ahead of time
Example: *Out of the blue HEAD CALM a letter from Lloyds of London demanding £10,000,000 from his Lordship END insisting AWN a settlement as HOURLY as poss*

The story so far ...

Lord P-H's creditors come out in force and he asks **Spraint** about filing for bankruptcy, while half-confiding in his lady wife: e.g., that various bits of the art collection will have to go. The castle itself is falling suddenly into disrepair and the milking herd is drying up. **Lord P-H** asks **Inspector Moleskin**, his friendly local plod, to keep an eye on the staff, who he fears are pilfering. Elsewhere, to the chagrin of all, **Daphne** has entered her Pekingese for Crufts. **Bunty**'s diet is not doing the trick, although **Rupert** is still pursuing her. **Harry** dreams of being knighted and keeps up the pressure on **Poppy**. The younger generation moan about corpulence and tattoos in certain sectors of lower class life. A new cocker appears for **Rupert** to 'train'. Then a thunderbolt: a hurricane has resulted in **Lord P-H** receiving a £10m bill from Lloyds of London.

I

IAN: (Preposition)
Meaning: Inside
Example: *Godfrey was adamant that the FILE HEAD been committed IAN the BAULKS BART the ref was blind END the penalty was not awarded*

INJURE: (Proper noun, place name)
Meaning: A large country BAY Pakistan
Example: *Lord P-H HEAD enormously enjoyed the old days IAN the officers' mess when serving IAN bomb disposal with the Royal Engineers IAN INJURE*

INFECT: (Conjunction)
Meaning: Really
Example: *His Lordship HEAD finally HEAD to confess confidentially to her Ladyship that they were INFECT somewhat deep IAN the CREPE financially*

INFLATE: (Noun)
Meaning: A publication
Example: *The younger cousins were so bored AWN the plane out to St Trop for their HAULS that they HEAD resorted to reading the INFLATE magazine*

INSANE: (Noun)
Meaning: An identifying board outside a pub

ISLE: (Noun)
Meaning: A nocturnal BARD
Example: *Rupert was lying awake dreaming of Bunty END listening to the distant hooting of an ISLE (**See also** PALAVER, SNAPE, SWORN)*

J

JAILS: (Proper noun, name)
Meaning: As IAN farmer

JARMIES: (Noun, plural)
Meaning: Pullovers, sweaters
Example: *Mrs Sloppetty HEAD always made sure to pack extra JARMIES for Rupert when he was sent off to Eton*

JAW: (Noun)
Meaning: French for day, one of two words retained BAY Rupert, often preceded BAY BORN

JEKYLL: (Noun)
Meaning: A wild dog
Example: *Lord P-H's creditors were closing IAN AWN him like a pack of hungry JEKYLLS*

JEMMY: (Proper noun, name)
Meaning: As IAN Clarkson, Paxman etc

JEST: (Adverb)
Meaning: Simply
Example: *"Aren't the geegees JEST too adorable!" exclaimed*

Daphne F-H IAN earshot of the entire Royal Family

JEWEL: (Noun)
Meaning: A FATE
Example: *Godfrey was seriously wondering if the only way out of his gambling debt was to consider suggesting a JEWEL*

JUGGLER: (Noun)
Meaning: A blood carrying device
Example: *If IAN any DIGHT Lady P-H always went straight for the JUGGLER*

JULIE: (Adverb)
Meaning: Officially, IAN a timely way
Example: *Godfrey replied IAN writing to his club that his bar bill being £4583 IAN the red was JULIE noted*

K

KALE: (Proper noun, name)
Meaning: A lower class name

KARL: (Noun)
Meaning: A wavy tress of hair
Example: *Priscilla JEST loved the little kiss KARL that flopped over the face of the new CAULKER*

KATE: (Noun)
Meaning: A flying toy
Example: *Despite her best efforts Priscilla HEAD CALM DINE to dinner already as HAY as a KATE*

KELLY: (Proper noun, place name)
Meaning: As IAN the main FAIRY port IAN Northern France

KELVIN: (Proper noun, name)
Meaning: Underwear
Example: *HAIRY F-H always made sure he HEAD particularly fresh KELVINS AWN if there was even the slightest chance of bumping into Poppy* (**See also** **PENCE**)

KEMPT: (Verb, past tense)
Meaning: IAN canvas accommodation
Example: *Bunty always KEMPT IAN the same place each year at Glastonbury*

KEN: (Verb)
Meaning: Synonym of CAIRN

KENDAL: (Noun)
Meaning: A taper
Example: *Despite herself Bunty HEAD FAINLY agreed to a KENDAL light dinner with Rupert*

KENNY: (Adjective)
Meaning: Shrewd
Example: *All HEAD to agree that Archie MacSporranhead stood out as being exceeding KENNY with money even amongst a race of spectacular tight arses*

KENYA: (Adjective)
Meaning: Comparative of KENNY

Despite her best efforts Priscilla HEAD CALM DINE to dinner already as HAY as a KATE

KENYAN: (Noun)
Meaning: A gorge, as IAN The Grand

KENT: (Proper noun, name)
Meaning: Somewhat BETTY psychoanalyst

KEPT: (Verb)
Meaning: Topped
Example: *Lord P-H felt the revelation from Inspector Moleskin that Snitcher END Spraint HEAD been pilfering really KEPT it all*

KERRY: (Verb)
Meaning: To bear or manhandle
Example: *"Snitcher looked distinctly surly when EH asked him to KERRY everyone's BEGS up to their rooms IAN the tower,"* complained Rupert

KETCH: (Noun)
Meaning: A trophy
Example: *If the castle HEAD to be sold to pay debts, Lord END Lady P-H feared that Rupert would no longer be the KETCH he once was*

KETCHUP: (Noun)
Meaning: Recorded media
Example: *Daphne F-H couldn't wait to get BECK to Chelsea END watch Eastenders AWN KETCHUP*

KETTERING: (Noun)
Meaning: Food
Example: *Everyone was forced to agree that they should have DARN something about Mrs Sloppetty's KETTERING years ago*

KETTLE: (Noun)
Meaning: A collection of bovines
Example: *Lord P-H was wondering about the poor price Snitcher HEAD apparently received for the KETTLE, END was this right?*

KLEIN: (Noun, Germanic extraction)
Meaning: A funny man at a circus
Example: *When END if the day should CALM, Rupert would not be the FAST KLEIN to run Hurtingseaux, thought his Lordship ruefully*

KNAVES: (Noun, plural)
Meaning: Sharp things
Example: *Godfrey began to fear that his gambling CHARMS really HEAD the KNAVES out for him*

KOREA: (Noun)
Meaning: Job direction
Example: *Rupert acknowledged to himself that taking over Hurtingseaux, if END when that time should CALM, was effectively going to be a full-time KOREA*

KORMA: (Noun)
Meaning: A piece of punctuation
Example: *Rupert could JEST about grasp the role of a full stop BART struggled enormously with the correct use of the KORMA*

KUWAIT: (Adverb)
Meaning: A form of emphatic agreement
Example: *Godfrey: "There seem to be a great many FETISH people at Wimbledon this year." Bunty: "KUWAIT."*

K

L

LABEL: (Noun)
Meaning: Written defamation
Example: *IAN EDITION to his other troubles, Lord P-H was now being sued for LABEL BAY Archie MacSporranhead for the HOBBLE comments written about him IAN the family history*

LACE: (Noun)
Meaning: Parasites
Example: *Priscilla reeled BECK IAN disgust as she was sure she HEAD seen that Snitcher HEAD LACE IAN his hair*

LAGER: (Noun)
Meaning: A type of barge-like working boat similar to a gaffer

LAKE: (Verb)
Meaning: To FEIGNED agreeable
Example: *"EH don't LAKE to be overdramatic BART EH am KUWAIT certain EH have ebola," said Lady P-H to Poppy, who sprang backwards*

LAME: (Noun)
Meaning: A green fruit
Example: *Bunty HEAD taken to adding a slice of LAME to her gin*

LANE: (Noun)
Meaning: A mark
Example: *Lord P-H was growing suspicious that Spraint was now helping himself to his brandy so he drew a secret LANE AWN the decanter to mark the level*

LARCH: (Noun)
Meaning: A sudden ungainly movement from one direction to another
Example: *Daphne F-H was proclaiming that the government needed a GOURD LARCH to the right END the sooner the better (**See also** TORTE, WARBLE)*

LARDER: (Adverb)
Meaning: Higher volume
Example: *To make a foreigner understand what she was saying Lady P-H simply repeated what she HEAD said previously, BART LARDER*

To make a foreigner understand what she was saying Lady P-H simply repeated what she HEAD said previously, BART LARDER

LARK: (Noun)
Meaning: Fortune
Example: *When Poppy appeared slightly drunk near HAIRY F-H's bedroom he thought his LARK might be IAN*

LARVA: (Noun)
Meaning: A paramour
Example: *Bunty HEAD*

FAINLY succumbed to dinner with Rupert who was explaining that it was OK for her to BECALM his LARVA even if they were FAST cousins, END that there was no chance of their offspring being at all BETTY

LASER: (Proper noun, name)
Meaning: As in Minnelli

LAST: (Noun)
Meaning: Carnal passion
Example: *HAIRY F-H was thinking to himself that LAST was a deadly sin END that he was really a very naughty boy*

LATE: (Noun)
Meaning: Illumination
Example: *HAIRY F-H turned DINE the LATE END whispered for Poppy to CALM IAN, which she did*

LAYER: (Noun)
Meaning: Teller of mistruths
Example: *It HEAD to be said that Godfrey was beginning to get a reputation as a bit of a LAYER*

LAZE: (Noun plural)
Meaning: Mistruths

LEAPT: (Verb, past tense)
Meaning: Drank
Example: *Up IAN Scotland, Archie MacSporranhead LEAPT up the news of all Lord P-H's troubles with considerable glee*

LED: (Noun)
Meaning: A young male
Example: *Godfrey HEAD been drinking heavily before settling DINE to one more game of poker with the LEDS*

LEGGING: (Noun)
Meaning: Insulation
Example: *The castle suddenly seemed to be falling apart END Lord P-H HEAD sent Snitcher up to the attic where the LEGGING was IAN a disastrous state of repair*

LEMMING: (Noun)
Meaning: Period of farming activity
Example: *Priscilla absolutely adored seeing the new arrivals IAN the field during the LEMMING season*

LEND: (Noun)
Meaning: GRIND
Example: *Lady P-H was never slow to tell people that the 5000 acres of LEND around Hurtingseaux Castle HEAD been IAN the family for over 500 years*

LENTERN: (Noun)
Meaning: A type of LATE
Example: *The sixteenth century LENTERN over the front gate HEAD mysteriously disappeared over night, presumed stolen*

LESS: (Noun)
Meaning: A young female
Example: *"Now be a GOURD LESS END let me really have it," said HAIRY F-H to Poppy as he produced a particularly swishy cane*

LETCH: (Noun)
Meaning: A door fastening device
Example: *HAIRY F-H explained to Poppy that he would now always leave the LETCH to his bedroom door off when staying at Hurtingseaux*

LETTUCE: (Noun)
Meaning: A garden erection
Example: *Lady P-H was*

ASHLEY KUWAIT admiring of the new LETTUCE that HEAD been put up for the roses to ramble over

LEVY: (Noun)
Meaning: WC
Example: *Lord P-H always judged it a GOURD night's sleep if he didn't have to go to the LEVY more than FAV times*

LIBYA: (Noun, plural)
Meaning: An unmentionable part of a lady's undercarriage

LIGHT: (Noun)
Meaning: A thug
Example: *Daphne F-H HEAD been accosted BAY a ghastly LIGHT selling the Big Issue outside South Ken station of all places*

LINE: (Noun)
Meaning: A large member of the cat family native to Africa

L

M

MACE: (Noun, plural)
Meaning: More than one small rodent
Example: *The castle's attics were BECALMING completely overrun BAY MACE (**See also** MICE)*

MAILED: (Adjective)
Meaning: Relatively weak
Example: *Lady P-H thought that morning that she HEAD perhaps developed a MAILED case of terminal cancer...*

MAIN: (Noun)
Meaning: A pit
Example: *...END she HEAD FINED the internet offered a MAIN of medical information AWN the subject to share with her DORK*

MAKE: (Noun)
Meaning: An amplification device
Example: *Daphne F-H was so drunk at the charity karaoke evening she was sick all over the MAKE*

MALE: (Noun)
Meaning: An imperial measure of distance
Example: *HAIRY F-H said the Aston was lucky to do fifteen MALES to the gallon*

MANED: (Noun)
Meaning: Brain
Example: *As his troubles mounted, Lord P-H thought he was going slowly out of his MANED*

MANY: (Proper noun, name)
Meaning: Famous French impressionist

MARCH: (Adjective)
Meaning: A lot
Example: *"Dearest Bunty, Please, oh please. MARCH love. Rupert XXXX"*

MARDI: (Adjective)
Meaning: Covered IAN wet earth
Example: *Daphne F-H HEAD stepped IAN a puddle END made her new Jimmy Choos all MARDI*

MARK: (Noun)

Meaning: Filth

Example: *It was an indisputable fact that Snitcher smelled strongly of MARK even after his monthly ablution*

MARQUEE: (Adjective)

Meaning: Covered IAN MARK

MARSHY: (Adjective)

Meaning: Pureed

Example: *All HEAD to agree that Mrs Sloppetty's MARSHY peas HEAD been an unqualified success*

MARY: (Verb)

Meaning: To wed

Example: *Bunty was beginning to think that if she were to own the castle it might ASHLEY not be KUWAIT so appalling to MARY Rupert*

MARTYR: (Verb)

Meaning: To speak quietly without making oneself CLAIRE

Example: *Disaster!!! MacSporranhead HEAD won the LABEL action END Sprint smiled as he heard Lord P-H start to MARTYR uncontrollably to himself*

MAST: (Verb)

Meaning: To be obliged to

Example: *"Everyone simply MAST CALM to our place IAN Val D'Isere next winter," said Daphne F-H IAN a LARD voice*

MASTERED: (Noun)

Meaning: A hot paste

Example: *The FRAYED tongue Mrs Sloppetty HEAD prepared for the picnic was only ingestible with lashings of MASTERED*

MATE: (Verb)

Meaning: Could possibly

Example: *Pigs MATE FLAY*

MATEY: (Adjective)

Meaning: Powerful

Example: *"HIGH are the MATEY fallen", mused his Lordship*

MAUDE: (Adjective)

Meaning: Shortened form of recent, as IAN MAUDE CORNS

M

MAUDLIN: (Noun)
Meaning: The act of being a CLOSE horse, posing for pictures
Example: *END to think that Priscilla HEAD HEAD a promising time MAUDLIN IAN London before she fell IAN with the wrong CRIED*

MAUL: (Proper noun, name)
Meaning: As IAN Flanders

MAY: (Possessive pronoun)
Meaning: Belonging to me

MAYORLY: (Adverb)
Meaning: Simply
Example: *Lady P-H was complaining to Poppy that the DORK HEAD dismissed her diagnosis of heart disease saying it was MAYORLY a case of indigestion*

MECCA: (Proper noun, name)
Meaning: As IAN that awful McCartney person

MED: (Adjective)
Meaning: Unhinged
Example: *The DORK said that if Priscilla didn't stop taking BEND substances she would very likely go MED (**See also MERDE**)*

MEDICINE: (Proper noun, place name)
Meaning: As IAN Square Gardens

MEDLEY: (Adverb)
Meaning: Uncontrollably
Example: *Rupert HEAD decided he really was now MEDLEY IAN love with Bunty's MANED as well as her BAWDY*

MEG: (Noun)
Meaning: A periodical
Example: *Mrs F-H was pleased that her own Knightsbridge HEISS HEAD featured IAN the society MEG Tatler, END Hurtingseaux Castle never HEAD*

MEL: (Noun)
Meaning: The Royal thoroughfare IAN front of Buckingham Palace

MELODY: (Noun)

Meaning: A sickness

Example: *Lady P-H HEAD awoken that morning with a particular MELODY that not even she could diagnose*

MEMBER: (Noun)

Meaning: A particularly HOBBLE snake

Example: *Lord P-H recalled he HEAD once shown considerable bravery diverting a black*

MEMBER which was planning to take a BAIT out of Her Ladyship's BAHT, an action that he subsequently often regretted (***See also*** **VAPOUR**)

MEMORIES: (Noun, plural)

Meaning: Breasts

Example: *HAIRY F-H HEAD always HEAD his EH AWN Poppy as he didn't care for fillies with small MEMORIES*

*Rupert HEAD decided he really was now **MEDLEY** IAN love with Bunty's MANED as well as her BAWDY*

MEN: (Noun)
Meaning: A single male human

MEND: (Verb, past tense)
Meaning: Armed
Example: *Lord P-H was hoping against hope that he was not going to have to sell Hurtingseaux to pay debts... he HEAD MEND the trenches before END he would do so again*

MENDABLE: (Noun)
Meaning: Lower jaw
Example: *In profile, Lady P-H was said to have a MENDABLE LAKE a hyena's*

MENTAL: (Noun)
Meaning: A cloak or garment
Example: *Blissfully ignorant of his father's fiscal predicament, Rupert was ASHLEY KUWAIT looking FORD to the challenge of taking up the Pails-Hurtingseaux MENTAL AWN the demise of his DEAD*

MENTION: (Noun)
Meaning: A large HEISS
Example: *HAIRY F-H was always slightly dismissive of Hurtingseaux, seeing it as more of a MENTION than an actual castle*

MENU: (Proper noun, name)
Meaning: A northern football club
Example: *Lady P-H detested all things football END especially MENU*

MERDE: (Adjective)
Meaning: Crazy, synonym of MED

MERLOT: (Adjective)
Meaning: Relaxed
Example: *Priscilla FINED her new supply of Moroccan grass made her feel particularly MERLOT* (**See also TRAIN**)

MERRY: (Proper noun, name)
Meaning: As IAN Queen of Scots, Berry etc

MESCALINE: (Adjective)
Meaning: Male
Example: *Rupert was experimenting with stubble to see if he could make himself appear more MESCALINE*

MESH: (Noun)
Meaning: A potato dish
Example: *Not even Mrs Sloppetty could mess up MESH*

MESS: (Noun)
Meaning: A lot
Example: *Spraint arrived that morning with what seemed a faint smile AWN his face END a silver tray AWN which were piled a MESS of bills for his Lordship*

MET: (Noun)
Meaning: A small carpet
Example: *The cat sat AWN the MET*

META: (Noun)
Meaning: An issue
Example: *Lady P-H was saying that having so many awful foreigners scrounging about the country was fast BECALMING a very serious META, very serious INFECT*

METHS: (Noun, plural)
Meaning: Arithmetic
Example: *Rupert was completely END ARTILY a non-starter at METHS*

MICE: (Noun)
Meaning: A small rodent
Example: *"CREPES! A MICE!" cried Rupert*

MIND: (Noun)
Meaning: A small MEN-made hillock
Example: *The original castle MIND HEAD been constructed IAN 1067*

MINI: (Adjective)
Meaning: A lot
Example: *"There are far too MINI immigrants IAN this country, especially IAN the health service," proclaimed Lady P-H*

MORLEY: (Proper noun, name)
Meaning: Girl's name as IAN Sugden

MORNAY: (Proper noun, name)
Meaning: Another famous French impressionist, friend of MANY

MORGUE: (Noun)
Meaning: A feline of dubious parentage

M

MORSE: (Noun)
Meaning: A spreading green plant
Example: *Up AWN the battlements Lord P-H END Snitcher saw the root of the damp problem – half of the roof was covered IAN a thick coating of oozing MORSE*

MORTALLY: (Adjective)
Meaning: Varied IAN appearance or character
Example: *Daphne F-H always felt the staff at Hurtingseaux to be a somewhat MORTALLY crew*

The story so far ...

Lord **P-H** tells **Lady P-H** of their predicament but keeps it from the children who remain in blissful ignorance. **Lady P-H**'s mood blackens. The castle attics are becoming overrun with mice and the roof is leaking badly. **Godfrey** gets into deeper trouble with his bookies. Surprisingly, **Bunty** has a change of heart and agrees to dinner, but dinner only, with **Rupert**, at which he explains that incest is a thing of the past. **Harry** has also scored with **Poppy**. The social scene continues at Wimbledon and **Daphne** invites everyone skiing the following winter. **Inspector Moleskin** confirms **Lord P-H**'s suspicions that **Snitcher** and **Spraint** are indeed pilfering. Just when it seems impossible for things to get worse, they do: **Lord P-H** loses a libel action brought against him by **Archie MacSporranhead** for defamation. However, we detect that while he is down he may not yet be out.

N

NAAN: (Noun)
Meaning 1: A Holy Sister

Meaning 2: Zero

NAIL: (Proper name place)
Meaning: A river IAN Egypt

NATALIE: (Adverb)
Meaning: Trim, smart
Example: *HAIRY F-H thought Poppy looked particularly NATALIE turned out that morning IAN her crispy-fresh maid's uniform*

NAUGHTY: (Adjective)
Meaning: Difficult to resolve
Example: *His Lordship was talking to Inspector Moleskin about the NAUGHTY situation he (his Lordship) FINED himself IAN... END whether he (Moleskin) could be of help IAN any further way*

NEIGH: (Adverb)
Meaning: Near
Example: *It was NEIGH to midnight END Rupert HEAD not yet tried to kiss Bunty*

NECK: (Noun)
Meaning: Special ability
Example: *Lord P-H always thought Daphne F-H HEAD the NECK of doing the wrong thing at the wrong time*

NET: (Noun)
Meaning: A small FLAY
Example: *That year's village barbecue HEAD been made even less tolerable BAY a swarm of HOBBLE BAITING NETS*

NEVILLE: (Noun)
Meaning: A part of the BAWDY
Example: *There were times when Lord P-H was so overwhelmed BAY his pending ruin that he could only sit there END gaze at his NEVILLE*

NICE: (Noun)
Meaning: Intelligence
Example: *It was clear to all who met him that Rupert was a pleasant enough BOARD BART one with exceeding little NICE*

N

NINE: (Noun)
Meaning: A part of speech
Example: *Rupert could JEST about identify a verb, BART a NINE was beyond him*

NIGH: (Adverb)
Meaning: At the present time
Example: *"NIGH is the winter of our discontent," thought Lord P-H*

NOUGHT: (Adverb)
Meaning: Negative
Example: *Godfrey told his bookmaker he was NOUGHT yet IAN the position to pay his gambling debts*

O

OARS: (Proper NINE, place name)
Meaning: A large antipodean LEND MESS

OBEYED: (Verb)
Meaning: To stand
Example: *If there was one word Lady P-H could NOUGHT OBEYED it was toilet… END its utterance was totally BEND at Hurtingseaux*

OPRAH: (NINE)
Meaning: Musical entertainment
Example: *Priscilla adored OPRAH, particularly when legless*

ORDER: (Adjective)
Meaning: Stranger
Example: *Lord P-H told Moleskin that Spraint END Snitcher's behaviour was getting ORDER END ORDER BAY the day*

ORDERLY: (Adverb)
Meaning: Strangely
Example: *Lord P-H repeated that Spraint END Snitcher were behaving more END more ORDERLY BAY the day*

ORF: (Preposition)
Meaning: Away. Normally preceded BAY any of the following: Get, Naff, Bugger … succeeded BAY… MAY LEND

ORLY: (Proper NINE, name)
Meaning: Short form of MEN'S name as IAN Twist, Reed, Murs, Preston

ORPHAN: (Adverb)
Meaning: KUWAIT a lot
Example: *Lord P-H ORPHAN wondered what he HEAD ever seen IAN his lady wife*

P

PAIL: (NINE)
Meaning 1: A large MENTION or stately home
Example: *HAIRY F-H was nevertheless happy to refer to Hurtingseaux Castle as a PAIL*

Meaning 2: A MELODY of the BECK passage
Example: *Predictably Lady P-H was a leading expert AWN PAILS*

PAIN: (Verb)
Meaning: To miss
Example: *Rupert HEAD again failed to score with Bunty END was NIGH beginning to PAIN for her*

PAINT: (NINE)
Meaning: A liquid quantity
Example: *Godfrey suggested discussing his growing gambling debts with his creditors over a quiet PAINT, which they refused*

PALAVER: (NINE)
Meaning: A type of BARD that CALMS IAN golden END grey varieties
Example: *Rupert HEAD*

O
P

accidently shot a golden PALAVER AWN the FAST drive one season right IAN front of Prince FLIP, The Duke of Edinburgh (**See also SNAPE, SWORN**)

PALTRY: (NINE)
Meaning: Domestic fowl
Example: *Lord P-H was remarking to Snitcher HIGH thin the PALTRY were looking END HIGH they HEAD started pecking one anothers' BALMS*

PAPER: (NINE)
Meaning: A musician
Example: *Archie MacSporranhead never did pay the PAPER*

PAR: (NINE)
Meaning: Force
Example: *"Where is Spraint when one needs him?" MARTYRED Lord P-H under his breath as he CLAIMED the ladder to the fuse BAULKS after a PAR CART*

PARADE: (NINE)
Meaning: Feeling of respect
Example: *The family were forced to recognise that, despite their revolting appearance, Mrs Sloppetty took great PARADE IAN her pig's trotter END beetroot rissoles*

PARCH: (NINE)
Meaning: A roosting place for a BARD
Example: *Lady P-H was convinced today was the FOETAL day when she would FAINLY fall ORF the PARCH*

PARK: (NINE)
Meaning: A small bonus
Example: *Spraint considered helping himself occasionally to a bottle of vintage BARBELS to be one of the MINI PARKS of the job*

PARLOUS: (Adjective)
Meaning: Having no PAR
Example: *Lady P-H was bemoaning the fact that the country seemed PARLOUS to prevent all those thousands of migrants swarming all over the place*

PARQUET: (Adjective)
Meaning: Coldish
Example: *HAIRY F-H told Poppy to jump BECK into BARED as it was a bit PARQUET without her*

PARSON: (NINE)
Meaning: A human being

PART: (NINE)
Meaning: A stroke IAN golf
Example: *Godfrey HEAD missed a simple big-money-winning PART AWN the 18th END broke his club over his knee*

PARTY: (NINE)
Meaning: A hardening sealant
Example: *Spraint HEAD reported that rain was pouring IAN upstairs as there was no PARTY IAN the windows*

PASS: (NINE)
Meaning: A yellowish bodily excretion
Example: *Remarkably she was still alive, BART Lady P-H HEAD FINED some interesting looking PASS oozing from somewhere BLOW*

PAUPER: (NINE)
Meaning: A stud fastening device
Example: *Bunty's DART HEAD NOUGHT gone as well as imagined END one of the PAUPERS AWN her jacket was about to CALM ORF*

PAWNED: (NINE)
Meaning: A small BAWDY of water
Example: *The DARK PAWNED at Hurtingseaux HEAD BECALM almost totally blanketed IAN weed that summer*

PAY: (NINE)
Meaning: A pastry
Example: *Even the new CAULKER HEAD turned its nose up at Mrs Sloppetty's attempt at nouvelle cuisine, a gizzard END sweetbread PAY*

PEAR: (NINE)
Meaning: A projection into the sea
Example: *When walking DINE the PEAR, Bunty FAINLY FINED herself slipping both her*

P

HENS into Rupert's, END agreed to MARY him

PECK: (Verb)
Meaning: To fill suitcases
Example: *Godfrey's creditors warned him against PECKING his BEGS END fucking ORF*

PEDAL: (NINE)
Meaning: A walk IAN water
Example: *Bunty END Rupert could NIGH be seen having a quick PEDAL AWN the beach*

PELE: (Adjective)
Meaning: Friendly
Example: *Daphne F-H HEAD clocked that husband HAIRY seemed to be getting distinctly PELE with Poppy*

PELLET: (NINE)
Meaning: Taste
Example: *Everyone wondered if INFECT there HEAD always been something wrong with Mrs Sloppetty's PELLET...*

PEN: (NINE)
Meaning: A cooking vessel
Example: *...END they similarly*

*agreed that it MATE be GOURD if she occasionally washed up her PENS (**See also** PORT)*

PENFUL: (Adjective)
Meaning: Hurting
Example: *Lady P-H was saying to Poppy HIGH PENFUL it was that the village NIGH HEAD a ghastly new-build HEISS, PECKED with appalling people*

PENCE: (Adjective)
Meaning: Underwear
Example: *Bunty said that it was absolute PENCE that she HEAD fallen ORF her horse that morning*

PENT: (Verb)
Meaning: Breathe deeply END quickly
Example: *The new CAULKER did nothing BART pee, poo END PENT*

PEPPER: (NINE)
Meaning: A publication
Example: *To economise, Lord P-H HEAD sadly cancelled The Sun, his daily PEPPER for the last 40 years*

PERISH: (NINE)
Meaning: Parochial
Example: *With harvest festival CALMING up Lord P-H HEAD been invited to read the lesson at the PERISH church*

PESTER: (NINE)
Meaning: Italian food stuff
Example: *Lady P-H abhorred END eschewed all foreign food END refused even to keep PESTER IAN the HEISS*

PESTLE: (NINE)
Meaning: A sweetie
Example: *Ever since his nursery days Rupert HEAD always carried a PECK of his favourite fruit PESTLES*

PET: (NINE)
Meaning: A tap
Example: *HAIRY F-H popped a fifty pound note IAN one of Poppy's HENS END gave her a friendly PET AWN the BALM*

PETTY: (NINE)
Meaning: A burger

Example: *Mrs Sloppetty was experimenting with a tripe PETTY*

PHONETICAL: (Adjective)
Meaning: Passionate
Example: *Rupert was NIGH PHONETICAL about getting Bunty into BARED, BART she wanted to wait until they HEAD gone DINE the AIL*

PINED: (NINE)
Meaning: British currency denomination (*See also* PINES)

PINES: (NINE plural)
Meaning: More than one PINED
Example: *Godfrey's tail was FARM between his legs as he asked his DEAD for one hundred thousand PINES to pay his debts, which HAIRY F-H flatly refused*

PLAQUE: (Verb)
Meaning: To remove feathers
Example: *The family agreed that Mrs Sloppetty HEAD NOUGHT KUWAIT got the hang of HIGH to successfully PLAQUE a BARD*

P

PLATE: (Adjective)
Meaning: Well mannered
Example: *Lady P-H was saying that it was a great pity Snitcher couldn't try being more PLATE JEST once IAN a while*

PLAYED: (Verb, past tense)
Meaning: To have been provided continuously with drink
Example: *It was CLAIRE from her dishevelled appearance at dinner that Priscilla HEAD PLAYED herself with BARBELS all afternoon*

PLAYERS: (NINE)
Meaning: A grasping tool
Example: *One of Godfrey's creditors HEAD him pinned DINE END was threatening to pull his front teeth out with a HOBBLE looking pair of rusty PLAYERS if he didn't CORFE up BAY next week*

PLOUGH: (Adjective)
Meaning: A side dish
Example: *Godfrey shuffled home despondently END all he could afford was a takeaway COWRI with PLOUGH rice*

POORLY: (Proper NINE, name)
Meaning: Popular name for a parrot

PORT: (NINE)
Meaning: A cooking vessel
Example: *Lord P-H was wandering with his gun IAN the wood END took a PORT shot at a passing BARD*

PORTABLE: (Adjective)
Meaning: Capable of going into a pocket
Example: *Godfrey HEAD snuck into his snooker club BART HEAD FINED that most balls were simply NOUGHT PORTABLE*

PORTHOLE: (NINE)
Meaning: A hole IAN the road
Example: *HAIRY F-H's suspension was NOUGHT up to the PORTHOLES IAN the Hurtingseaux drive*

It was simply NOUGHT possible to be PORTIA than a Pails-Hurtingseaux

PORTIA: (Adjective, comparative)
Meaning: To be more upmarket
Example: *It was simply NOUGHT possible to be PORTIA than a Pails-Hurtingseaux*

PORTER: (Verb)
Meaning: To wander about doing small jobs
Example: *To take his MANED ORF things His Lordship HEAD begun to PORTER about IAN his cellar*

POURED: (NINE)
Meaning: The outer casing of peas
Example: *HAIRY F-H was saying to Poppy that he felt they were two peas IAN a POURED*

PRAIRIE: (NINE)
Meaning: A religious HEISS, rather LAKE a monastery
Example: *Lady P-H was bemoaning the fact IAN a LARD voice that a ghastly family of arrivistes HEAD JEST bought the PRAIRIE DINE AWN the other side of the village*

P

PRAISE: (Verb)
Meaning: To lever
Example: *Godfrey HEAD failed to pay, so his creditors held him DINE END began to PRAISE out his front tooth with the HOBBLE pair of rusty PLAYERS*

PRAISE: (NINE)
Meaning: An award
Example: *Unfortunately for Rupert there HEAD been no PRAISE at Eton for being as thick as shit*

PRAY: (Verb)
Meaning: To snoop
Example: *Priscilla told her father that she didn't want to PRAY BART was everything OK with the family finances, to which His Lordship made a small CORFE before replying that all was JEST FEIGN END ticketty boo*

PRAYER: (Preposition)
Meaning: Before
Example: *Lord P-H was trying to remember the happy days at Hurtingseaux PRAYER to all*

the awful Horlicks he NIGH FINED himself IAN

PRET: (NINE)
Meaning: An idiot
Example: *Bunty was trying to concentrate AWN the castle END the money rather than the PRET she was due to MARY*

PRIDE: (Adjective)
Meaning: Feeling deep pleasure or affection
Example: *It HEAD to be said that, try as he MATE, Lord P-H was NOUGHT overly PRIDE of his offspring*

PRIOR: (NINE)
Meaning: An outcast
Example: *Lord P-H was BECALMING increasingly concerned that with the impending END inevitable loss of Hurtingseaux he MATE FEIGNED himself a social PRIOR, totally ostracised END never again invited to take a few PORTS at BARDS, read the lesson, open the village fete, or play CENTRE at Christmas*

PROLE: (NINE)
Meaning: A period of release from prison
Example: *Spraint was helpfully explaining to Lord P-H that IAN the event of default he MATE expect PROLE after he HEAD served a minimum of say 10 years*

PSALM: (Adjective)
Meaning: A few
Example: *Godfrey NIGH knew without DIGHT he really was IAN PSALM CANED of really deep CREPE*

Q

QUA: (NINE)
Meaning: A group of singers
Example: *Priscilla END Poppy HEAD agreed to dress the QUA stalls for the Harvest Festival that year*

QUARK: (NINE)
Meaning: An abnormality
Example: *His Lordship HEAD always hoped against hope that Rupert's stupidity was JEST a*

QUARK that he would grow out of

QUENELLE: (NINE)
Meaning: A MEN-made stretch of water
Example: *IAN the latest Tatler Daphne F-H HEAD spotted a pleasantly large villa for sale near the QUENELLE du Midi, END was considering making an EDITION to her collection*

Q

R

RACE: (NINE)
Meaning: A cereal
Example: *Mrs Sloppetty's RACE pudding was indistinguishable from cement*

RADA: (NINE)
Meaning: A nautical steering device
Example: *HAIRY F-H was proclaiming at the Royal Yacht Squadron bar that he would have won the CARP HEAD his RADA NOUGHT sheared ORF*

RAFT: (Verb, past tense)
Meaning: To have been physically intimidated
Example: *Godfrey HEAD been RAFT up before BART NOUGHT as BED as this*

RAID: (NINE)
Meaning: The act of being astride a horse
Example: *Despite her obvious END understandable misgivings Bunty was nevertheless wondering about what sort of RAID Rupert MATE be*

*Mrs Sloppetty's **RACE** pudding was indistinguishable from cement*

HAIRY F-H was
RALLY RALLY
extremely surprised
when his lady wife
caught him AWN the
job with Poppy

RAIDER: (Proper NINE, name)
Meaning: Sponsor of a golfing competition
Example: *Godfrey HEAD still NOUGHT learnt, END HEAD JEST lost a tidy PSALM AWN the RAIDER CARP*

RAIN: (Proper NINE, place name)
Meaning: A big river IAN Germany

RAINED: (NINE)
Meaning: The outer skin of cheese
Example: *Lady P-H HEAD told Mrs Sloppetty that she did NOUGHT wish to be FARCI, BART she should NOUGHT use the RAINED IAN the cheese omelette, particularly if Snitcher HEAD HEAD his MARDI HENS AWN it*

RALLY: (Adverb)
Meaning: Very
Example: *HAIRY F-H was RALLY RALLY extremely surprised when his lady wife caught him AWN the job with Poppy (**See also** RARELY, VARY)*

RAPE: (Adjective)
Meaning: Mature
Example: *Rupert was dejectedly relating that Snitcher HEAD said that the crops were still NOUGHT RAPE END would prob JEST DAY IAN the field*

R

RARE: (Verb)
Meaning: To bring up
Example: *Lord P-H knew his main duty was to RARE a suitable heir END preferably a spare, neither of which he felt he HEAD RALLY satisfactorily achieved*

RAREBIT: (NINE)
Meaning: More serious name for a BARNEY

RARELY: (Adverb)
Meaning: Synonym of RALLY (*See also* VARY)

RATE: (Adjective)
Meaning: Correct
Example: *Daphne F-H thought it only RATE to serve immediate divorce papers AWN HAIRY END take him to the cleaners for all she could...*

RATING: (NINE)
Meaning: Caligraphy
Example: *... END that she would be RATING immediately to Messrs Sue, Fleece END Fuckham of Lincoln's IAN*

RATIO: (Proper NINE, name)
Meaning: As IAN Nelson, another of Lord P-H's heroes

RAVEN: (Adjective)
Meaning: Screaming
Example: *IAN their separate ways Lord P-H, Lady P-H, HAIRY F-H END Godfrey all thought the world HEAD RALLY gone ARTILY RAVEN MERDE*

RAZOR: (NINE)
Meaning: Someone who gets up
Example: *Priscilla could never RARELY been described as an HOURLY RAZOR*

READILY: (Proper NINE, place name)
Meaning: A private school
Example: *Rupert went to Eton because he was too stupid to get into READILY*

REBEL: (NINE)
Meaning: A rough CRIED
Example: *It was Goodwood week END Rupert was complaining about the unspeakable REBEL in Non Members'*

RED: (NINE)
Meaning: A heating device
Example: *To save money Lord P-H HEAD turned ORF the RED IAN his room, BART was unaware that Spraint HEAD turned his own up*

REDDISH: (NINE)
Meaning: A salad vegetable
Example: *Lady P-H was cheered up briefly when her REDDISH surprisingly won FAST PRAISE at the village show*

REDNESS: (NINE)
Meaning: Being alert
Example: *When His Lordship was serving with great distinction IAN INJURE he was always IAN a state of permanent REDNESS*

REF: (Proper NINE, name)
Meaning: The FLAYING part of HM Armed Forces
Example: *HAIRY F-H HEAD liked to give the impression he HEAD been a pilot IAN the REF, BART NIGH his plane HEAD definitely suffered a major CRECHE*

Rupert was complaining about the unspeakable REBEL in Non Members'

When His Lordship was serving with great distinction IAN INJURE he was always IAN a state of permanent REDNESS

REGS: (NINE)
Meaning: Old CLOSE
Example: *Lord P-H was ruing his imminent fall from riches to REGS*

REMAINDER: (NINE)
Meaning: A chase up
Example: *That very morning his Lordship received a strongly worded REMAINDER from Lloyds of London to pay up or else*

RENT: (NINE)
Meaning: A LARD complaint
Example: *HAIRY F-H was having a RENT at his lawyer about PSALM pre-nup his estranged lady wife HEAD dug out*

REP: (NINE)
Meaning: A type of music
Example: *Priscilla FINED a decent snort of coke was the only thing that RALLY got her into REP*

REPLAY: (VERB)

Meaning: Respond

Example: *"Tell HAIRY to make the cheque out to MAY maiden name," said Daphne F-H in REPLAY to a question from Messrs Sue, Fleece END Fuckham of Lincoln's IAN*

RETARD: (Verb, past tense)

Meaning: No longer working

Example: *Lord P-H HEAD always PAINED for the simple life at Hurtingseaux after he HEAD RETARD having DARN his duty to his country*

RHETT: (NINE)

Meaning: A rodent, a bit LAKE a MICE

Example: *Lord P-H declared that Archie MacSporranhead was the most HOBBLE RHETT ever to crawl upon the earth*

RIGHT: (NINE)

Meaning: An utter defeat

Example: *To make things worse for Godfrey, England HEAD JEST been beaten BAY Scotland 54 – 13 at Twickers, a complete END utter RIGHT*

RIND: (Adjective)

Meaning: Circular

Example: *Bunty END Rupert HEAD gone ORF to Hatton Garden to FEIGNED something RIND END gold to put AWN her finger*

RITUALIST: (Proper NINE, title of publication)

Meaning: An annual list of the exceedingly EFFLUENT

Example: *Daphne F-H was consulting the Sunday Times RITUALIST to FEIGNED a suitable replacement husband*

ROARED: (NINE)

Meaning: An angling item

Example: *Lord P-H was wondering morosely if he would ever afford a ROARED AWN the TEST again*

RUSH-HOUR: (Proper NINE, place name)

Meaning: A large country around Moscow

Example: *Lady P-H HEAD never met any BAWDY from RUSH-HOUR BART knew she would detest them if she did*

R

The story so far ...

Something is rotten in the state of Hurtingseaux. The annual barbie is ruined by gnats, chickens eat each other, crops die in the fields, power cuts abound and, horror, new-builds are popping up in the village. **Lord P-H** is stunned into temporary depression but as an economy measure he cancels The Sun. **Godfrey**'s pleas to his creditors have failed and he has had his front teeth extracted. Uncharacteristically, **Priscilla** asks her father if everything is okay financially, etc. **Lord P-H** lies that all is fine, so the outer family continue with their frolics. Indeed **Rupert** and **Bunty** have agreed to tie the knot, although much to **Rupert**'s frustration there is no hanky-panky allowed prior. **Daphne** has been house hunting in the society mags and, by a stroke of good fortune, has caught **Harry** in flagrante with **Poppy**, thus allowing her to serve immediate divorce papers and go shopping.

S

SADE: (NINE)
Meaning: A team
Example: *Godfrey HEAD thought it the best England SADE for years, END practically unbeatable*

SAID: (Adjective)
Meaning: Unhappy
Example: *Lord P-H was walking about MARTYRING that it was a SAID day for Hurtingseaux*

SANE: (Verb)
Meaning: To place a signature AWN
Example: *Spraint HEAD shown IAN the MEN from the estate agents who asked Lord P-H to SANE at the bottom of their pro forma to put Hurtingseaux AWN the market*

SARI: (Proper NINE, place name)
Meaning: A county south of London

Example: *Lady P-H abominated SARI, a place overflowing with footballers END their ghastly wives*

SARK: (Verb)
Meaning: To draw IAN
Example: *Godfrey did have to admit that life RALLY did SARK as he examined the RARELY PENFUL gap IAN his front teeth*

SARNIE: (Adjective)
Meaning: BERATE, without a CLYDE IAN the sky
Example: *Priscilla dropped a few tabs END everything was SARNIE END FEIGN*

SATE: (NINE)
Meaning: A scene
Example: *Godfrey RALLY was a SATE for sore EHS*

SAY: (NINE)
Meaning: A resigned expulsion of breath
Example: *Hurtingseaux Castle HEAD been quickly bought BAY an anonymous buyer from Scotland END Lord P-H began*

to SANE the sale documents with a tearful SAY

SCARPER: (Verb)
Meaning: To sink
Example: *His Lordship was ashamed to admit that he MATE NIGH be totally END ARTILY SCARPERED*

SCHNELL: (Proper NINE, name)
Meaning: A haute couture brand
Example: *Bunty HEAD decided to wear SCHNELL at the wedding END was ORF to see her DEAD about paying for it*

SCORCH: (NINE)
Meaning: A drink
Example: *Lord P-H SET DINE AWN his own IAN his cellar END opened a bottle of SCORCH*

SCORN: (NINE)
Meaning: A type of BARN
Example: *AWN the way home Rupert END Bunty stopped at a darling little tea shop END HEAD a SCORN with GEM*

S

SEAN: (Verb, past tense)
Meaning: To have shined
Example: *Up IAN Scotland, Archie MacSporranhead congratulated himself AWN making hay while the sun SEAN*

SEB: (NINE)
Meaning: A disruptive PARSON at a hunt
Example: *Bunty was saying to Rupert HIGH beastly rude a SEB HEAD been to her last season...*

SEC: (NINE)
Meaning: A large BEG
Example: *... BART Rupert wasn't RARELY listening to Bunty – his only thought was about getting her into the SEC*

SECT: (Verb, past tense)
Meaning: Fired
Example: *Lady P-H was saying that one of her DORKS did NOUGHT agree with her own diagnosis END that it RARELY MAST be time that he was SECT*

SEND: (NINE)
Meaning: As IAN what you FEIGNED AWN the beach

Example: *Lord P-H could feel the SEND shifting quickly beneath his feet*

SENTRY: (Adjective)
Meaning: Relating to health
Example: *Lady P-H's gynaecologist was saying that her personal SENTRY hygiene was ASHLEY KUWAIT acceptable*

SET: (Verb)
Meaning: As IAN the cat SET AWN the MET

SEWERS: (Proper NINE, place name)
Meaning: Place IAN Egypt
Example: *Lord P-H remembered the SEWERS crisis only too well*

SEX: (NINE)
Meaning 1: A brass instrument
Example: *At Ronnie Scott's that night Priscilla HEAD never heard the SEX played with such passion*

Meaning 2: BEGS for coal

SHAH: (NINE)
Meaning: A quick precipitation

SHARD: (Verb)
Meaning: To wash
Example: *Bunty HEAD SHARD END was NIGH rubbing SCHNELL all over her BAWDY*

SHARE: (Adjective)
Meaning: Blatant
Example: *Lord P-H fumed that paying the agents such a large commission AWN £10 mill for the castle was SHARE daylight robbery*

SHARED: (NINE)
Meaning: An outbuilding
Example: *His Lordship heard from Inspector Moleskin that Snitcher END Spraint HEAD been plotting something IAN the garden SHARED, END that it possibly involved Archie MacSporranhead...of all people*

SHECKEL: (NINE)
Meaning: An iron fastening
Example: *Daphne F-H was delighted to at last be throwing ORF the SHECKEL of being married to HAIRY*

SHELL: (Verb)
Meaning: Will
Example: *"EH SHELL be avenged!" said Lord P-H to Moleskin IAN a LARD voice*

SHELLEY: (NINE)
Meaning: An alpine HEISS
Example: *HAIRY F-H was very much hoping that his estranged wife would somehow forget about her share IAN the SHELLEY IAN Val D'Isere*

SHITE: (Verb)
Meaning: To raise one's voice to make it LARDER
Example: *Lord P-H was NOUGHT one to get over-angry BART sometimes he felt he could SHITE at Rupert for NOUGHT being JEST a soupçon BERATER*

SHORED: (Adjective)
Meaning: Having shoes AWN
Example: *Bunty was going hunting the next day END asked Snitcher to ensure her mount was newly SHORED*

S

SHORT: (NINE)
Meaning: The discharge of a gun
Example: *Daphne F-H left her lawyers END was ORF to St Tropez LAKE a SHORT*

SIGNED: (NINE)
Meaning: A noise
Example: *Bunty sidled up to Rupert END could almost hear the SIGNED of the keys to the castle dropping into her lap*

SIMLA: (Adjective)
Meaning: Like
Example: *Godfrey's creditors HEAD said that if he ever failed to CORFE up again something SIMLA to what HEAD happened to his teeth would happen to his bollocks*

SKETCHLEY: (Adverb)
Meaning: Faintly
Example: *HAIRY F-H could only SKETCHLEY remember what he HEAD agreed IAN the pre-nup, BART he HEAD to admit it did INFECT look pretty BED...*

SLATE: (Adjective)
Meaning: Small
Example: *...though there was still a SLATE chance she MATE NOUGHT FEIGNED his ORF shore account*

SLAVER: (NINE)
Meaning: Oral moisture
Example: *Lady P-H insisted to her DORK that a simple SLAVER test would confirm her own diagnosis*

SLAY: (Adjective)
Meaning: Cunning
Example: *"EH may have the BAWDY of an avuncular old fool BART EH have the MANED of a SLAY old FORKS," thought Lord P-H to himself IAN the mirror as his revenge plan started to take shape*

SLEPT: (Verb)
Meaning: To have hit
Example: *Snitcher HEAD CALM into the drawing room IAN his MARDI boots END rather rudely SLEPT an unpaid bill for manure AWN the table*

Godfrey's creditors HEAD said that if he ever failed to CORFE up again something SIMLA to what HEAD happened to his teeth would happen to his bollocks

SMARTIE: (Adjective)
Meaning: Coarse
Example: *Rupert HEAD still NOUGHT FINED out HIGH SMARTIE Bunty MATE turn out to be IAN the SEC*

SNAPE: (NINE)
Meaning: A small wading BARD
Example: *His Lordship noticed a wisp of SNAPE LEND AWN the DARK PAWNED END took this as a positive omen*

SNORT: (NINE)
Meaning: Nasal mucus
Example: *Godfrey HEAD turned into a quivering wreck END was last seen crying IAN the street with SNORT CALMING out of his nose*

SPACE: (NINE)
Meaning: A culinary ingredient
Example: *Rupert HEAD SHARD, END was rubbing Old SPACE all over his BAWDY, END jumping about IAN pain*

S

SPAIN: (NINE)
Meaning: Bones that run up the BECK
Example: *Lord P-H simply did NOUGHT yet have the SPAIN to tell the children that he HEAD put the castle up for sale END that the family would soon be ruined END out AWN its AIR*

SPAKE: (Verb)
Meaning: To add a MANED bending substance covertly to
Example: *Priscilla was always KUWAIT pleased if she FINED PSALM CANED PARSON HEAD tried to SPAKE her drink*

SPATE: (NINE)
Meaning: A show of nastiness
Example: *As she left for the airport Daphne F-H HEAD keyed the Aston out of SHARE SPATE*

SPENDERS: (NINE)
Meaning: Device for holding things up
Example: *Rupert HEAD slid unseen into Ann Summers END was BAYING Bunty a pair of SPENDERS*

SPEY: (NINE)
Meaning: A secret observer
Example: *Lord P-H, concealed outside the SHARED with Moleskin, was horrified to overhear Spraint AWN the mobile to Archie MacSporranhead, who it turned out was the anonymous buyer of the castle: his own butler was a traitor END a damned SPEY to boot*

SPICE: (NINE)
Meaning: To whom one is married
Example: *Lady P-H was his Lordship's one END only SPICE, something he RARELY rather regretted (**See also** WAIF)*

SPITE: (Verb)
Meaning: To gush
Example: *Godfrey HEAD NIGH been confined to a MERDE HEISS where he would SPITE random bollocks*

SPRITES: (NINE)
Meaning: Vegetables
Example: *Mrs Sloppetty's SPRITES at Christmas always exceeded the very worst of expectations*

SPORT: (NINE)
Meaning: A small boil
Example: *Lady P-H HEAD JEST FINED a dangerous looking SPORT END was reaching for the internet*

SQUARE: (NINE)
Meaning: Minor landed gentleman
Example: *Lord P-H was always deeply irked if anyone referred to him JEST as a country SQUARE*

STAFF: (Verb)
Meaning: To thrust into
Example: *HEAD Lord P-H known that the anonymous buyer of Hurtingseaux was NAAN other than Archie MacSporranhead ...he would have told him to STAFF it up his BALM. BART, alas, Spraint HEAD concealed the truth END the contract HEAD been exchanged*

Lady P-H was his Lordship's one END only SPICE, something he RARELY rather regretted

S

Snitcher END Spraint HEAD abandoned the castle that morning END STARK two fingers up at an astonished Lady P-H, who thought she would DAY AWN the SPORT

STALE: (NINE)
Meaning: Fashion
Example: *Bunty was already thinking about the STALE of lettering for the wedding invitation*

STALKING: (NINE)
Meaning: Clothing for the leg
Example: *Rupert was hoping to unhook each STALKING individually from Bunty's SPENDERS with his teeth*

STARLING: (Proper NINE, place name)
Meaning: A town IAN Scotland from whence Archie MacSporranhead would be triumphantly moving South to

clean Lord P-H out END take possession of Hurtingseaux Castle

STARK: (Verb, past tense)
Meaning: Raised
Example: *Snitcher END Spraint HEAD abandoned the castle that morning END STARK two fingers up at an astonished Lady P-H, who thought she would DAY AWN the SPORT*

STARRED: (NINE)
Meaning: A stallion
Example: *Bunty was pretty sure Rupert would be a let-down END she would have to FEIGNED herself a secret STARRED when they were married*

STARTER: (NINE)
Meaning: Speaking IAN fits END starts
Example: *Godfrey HEAD lost all sanity as well as teeth END now spoke nothing BART gibberish with a noticeable STARTER*

STAY: (NINE)
Meaning: A pig's abode
Example: *Lord P-H was MARTYRING that if Snitcher END Spraint were freezing END naked END HEAD CALM begging for a BARED for the night he would NOUGHT even offer them a STAY*

STEFFI: (NINE)
Meaning: A breed of DINE market fighting dog
Example: *Bunty said that the SEB who HEAD been rude to her owned a particularly vicious little STEFFI with noticeably prominent balls*

STORK: (NINE)
Meaning: Equity
Example: *HAIRY F-H's lawyer said he HEAD instructed his broker to sell his entire STORK as well as the Aston – to pay the divorce settlement*

HAIRY F-H's lawyer said he HEAD instructed his broker to sell his entire STORK as well as the Aston – to pay the divorce settlement

SWAIN: (NINE)
Meaning: A pig
Example: *MARCH to her own surprise, Lady P-H's self-diagnosis that she HEAD somehow contracted human SWAIN flu turned out to be RATE*

SWORD: (NINE)
Meaning: A cur, bugger
Example: *Lord P-H finally decided that he himself HEAD been a bit of a SWORD not*

telling the children about the sale of the castle END the treachery of Spraint END Snitcher, END resolved to call a family meeting forthwith

SWORN: (NINE)
Meaning: A white BARD
Example: *Before the planned meeting Priscilla was out AWN the PAWNED IAN the boat drifting with a single SWORN*

T

TAIL: (NINE)
Meaning: Something you CARVER a roof with
Example: *Lord P-H was NIGH NOUGHT too concerned that a few TAILS MATE be missing AWN the roof, INFECT the more the merrier*

TALK: (NINE)
Meaning: A horological noise
Example: *As he planned his revenge, His Lordship was pacing his Hall where the grandfather*

clock went tick followed BAY its reassuring TALK

TAME: (NINE)
Meaning: When something happens
Example: *Bunty was thinking about what TAME the wedding should take place...*

TAPE: (NINE)
Meaning: Writing
Example: *... END what STALE of TAPE the invite should have*

MacSporranhead was unaware of Moleskin tailing him AWN the train END was uncharacteristically offering Spraint END Snitcher a wee TAUGHT of SCORCH, for free

TAR: (NINE)

Meaning: A HAY fortified building

Example: *Lord P-H made the CLAIM to the top of his TAR to think... END the plan to avenge himself AWN MacSporranhead, Spraint END Snitcher HEAD finally BECALM CLAIRE*

TARN: (NINE)

Meaning: A revolution

Example: *As part of his revenge plan Lord P-H HEAD sent Moleskin north to tail MacSporranhead END see if he could help TARN the tables*

TARRED: (Adjective)

Meaning: Exhausted

Example: *Lady P-H's latest MELODY HEAD rendered her too TARRED even to DAHL the DORK*

TATE: (Adjective)

Meaning: Miserly

Example: *Moleskin (NIGH IAN the train from Scotland south) TOLD His Lordship that despite MacSporranhead's new-FINED wealth he was still so TATE he was travelling second class*

TAUGHT: (NINE)

Meaning: A dram

Example: *MacSporranhead was*

unaware of Moleskin tailing him AWN the train END was uncharacteristically offering Spraint END Snitcher a wee TAUGHT of SCORCH, for free

TAY: (NINE)
Meaning: A cravate
Example: *As he was BECK IAN military mode finessing his plan, Lord P-H decided to dispense with the need to wear a TAY to dinner that evening*

TEARABLE: (Adjective)
Meaning: Very BED
Example: *HAIRY F-H HEAD decided that his position was INFECT so TEARABLE he HEAD to take his own life*

TECHI: (Adjective)
Meaning: Naff
Example: *Bunty END Rupert*

*Lady P-H was feeling a **TED** worse that morning END HEAD gone a dodgy shade of yellow*

agreed that any gold embossing AWN the invite would be JEST too TECHI for words

TECHS: (NINE)
Meaning: Government money as IAN income, corporation, evasion, return etc

TED: (NINE)
Meaning: A little
Example: *Lady P-H was feeling a TED worse that morning END HEAD gone a dodgy shade of yellow*

TELLY: (NINE)
Meaning: Amount
Example: *Rupert was telling Bunty HIGH MARCH he was looking FORD to the season END HIGH he END his DEAD HEAD SHORT 214 BARDS AWN the FAST drive last year, NOUGHT a BED TELLY BAY modern standards, what?*

TEMPER: (Verb)
Meaning: To fiddle
Example: *Moleskin wired through to His Lordship that Archie MacSporranhead was*

giving Spraint END Snitcher a lesson AWN HIGH to TEMPER with TECHS returns

TEND: (Verb, past tense)
Meaning: Having gone BRINE
Example: *Bunty was looking FORD to getting gloriously TEND IAN Mauritius AWN honeymoon*

TENURE: (Proper NINE, name)
Meaning: A girl's name

TERRACED: (NINE)
Meaning: A violent political activist
Example: *Lady P-H was totally END ARTILY CLAIRE IAN her own MANED that every Arab was a TERRACED*

TERRY: (Verb)
Meaning: To hang about
Example: *HAIRY F-H told Poppy that losing all his money was too HOBBLE for words, END that he could TERRY no longer IAN this world, to which Poppy agreed*

TEXT: (Verb, past tense)
Meaning: To have been fleeced BAY the government
Example: *Inspector Moleskin was keeping a close EH AWN Archie MacSporranhead END pricked up his AIRS AWN HERRING that he HEAD somehow avoided being TEXT all his life*

THEN: (Subordinating conjunction)
Meaning: Than

For his mother's funeral Rupert HEAD decided AWN a dark morning suit END a shiny, black TORPOR, which, usefully, he would also wear to his wedding

THRESH: (Verb)
Meaning: To move around uncontrollably
Example: *Lady P-H suddenly started to THRESH about IAN her BARED END then surprised Poppy BAY deciding to DAY*

TICKLY: (Adverb)
Meaning: Specially
Example: *AWN HERRING the commotion, Rupert HEAD dashed to his deceased mother's BARED END HEAD to agree that she did look TICKLY unwell*

TILE: (NINE)
Meaning: A cloth
Example: *Lord P-H came IAN END decided to CARVER his late SPICE'S face with a bathroom TILE*

TINE: (NINE)
Meaning: A residential area
Example: *With the divorce settlement IAN the BEG Daphne F-H decided to MARY an Arab END move to an even more expensive part of TINE.*

Thereafter, she was never seen again as she was forced after FAV minutes to wear a BARKER

TORPOR: (NINE)
Meaning: A distinctive piece of headgear
Example: *For his mother's funeral Rupert HEAD decided AWN a dark morning suit END a shiny, black TORPOR, which, usefully, he would also wear to his wedding*

TORTE: (Verb)
Meaning: To be unsteady
Example: *Apparently HAIRY F-H HEAD been seen BAY a local PARSON to TORTE briefly with Poppy at Beachy Head PRAYER to them both CLAIMING BECK into a car to take the final, FOETAL plunge over the cliff edge (**See also** WARBLE)*

TOURED: (NINE)
Meaning: Own
Example: *Lord P-H was KUWAIT looking FORD to sleeping AWN his TOURED in future*

TOURNIQUET: (Adjective)
Meaning: Tasting of Schweppes
Example: *After her mother's BERYL Priscilla was saying to the barman her drink was JEST perfect: "NOUGHT too ginny END NOUGHT too TOURNIQUET."*

TRADE: (Verb, past tense)
Meaning: To have HEAD a go
Example: *Rupert TRADE to put a brave face AWN things*

TRAIN: (Adjective)
Meaning: Descriptor of TAPE of white wine made near Tours

After her mother's BERYL Priscilla was saying to the barman her drink was JEST perfect: "NOUGHT too ginny END NOUGHT too TOURNIQUET."

TRAWL: (NINE)
**Meaning: An anonymous
FILE mouthed SWAIN
AWN the internet**

TRAY: (Verb)
Meaning: To attempt
Example: *Lord P-H HEAD
told Rupert END Priscilla that
they all HEAD to TRAY to
KERRY AWN regardless after
their mother's SAID death*

TRAYFUL: (NINE)
Meaning: A small thing
Example: *The next day, everyone
was more THEN a TRAYFUL
upset to hear FAST of the deaths
of HAIRY F-H END Poppy...
END then of Godfrey!!! also BAY
his own HENS apparently*

TREAD: (Adjective)
Meaning: Old fashioned

Example: *However, Priscilla was
getting over everything with a
joint END a bit of TREAD jazz
at Ronnie's*

TREK: (NINE)
Meaning: A path
Example: *Meanwhile, Inspector
Moleskin was well AWN TREK.
He HEAD told his Lordship of
MacSporranhead's failure to be
TEXT all his life END Lord P-H
was AWN the phone LAKE a
SHORT to his CHARM at HM
Revenue END Customs to lay the
META before him*

TRITE: (NINE)
Meaning: A fish
Example: *AWN a LATER
note, Rupert HEAD somehow
managed to KETCH a TRITE
that Mrs Sloppetty HEAD
broiled for supper*

U

UMBRAGE: (Proper NINE,
place name)
**Meaning: Where The Archers
takes place**

U

V

VACANT: (NINE)
Meaning: A rank of nobility
Example: *With all this death IAN the family Rupert was beginning to think he MATE INFECT BECALM a VACANT sooner rather THEN later*

VAIN: (NINE)
Meaning: A plant
Example: *The long awaited meeting to tell the family: His Lordship HEAD FAINLY begun his talk with Rupert, Bunty END Priscilla BAY explaining, IAN a roundabout way, that the Pails-Hurtingseaux grapes MATE unfortunately be about to wither AWN the VAIN...*

VAPOUR: (NINE)
Meaning: A snake
Example: *... END that the litigious Scottish VAPOUR Archie MacSporranhead was the new owner of Hurtingseaux...*

VARLET: (Adjective)
Meaning: A CARLA of the rainbow

Example: *During the meeting His Lordship's face HEAD gone almost VARLET with rage*

VARY: (Adverb)
Meaning: Synonym of RALLY END RARELY
Example: *To break the shocked silence Rupert said things looked VARY BED, after Mama deciding to DAY, END Godfrey, END HAIRY END Poppy. END Sprint END Snitcher deserting, END everything...*

VAULT: (NINE)
Meaning: A quantity of electricity
Example: *... Bunty added that she would happily apply a million VAULTS to the end of Archie MacSporranhead's sausage...*

VEIL: (Adjective)
Meaning: Disgusting
Example: *... all agreed that he was a RARELY VEIL Scotsman, BART what could be DARN?*

VESSEL: (NINE)
Meaning: A subject
Example: ... *IAN REPLAY to*
Bunty, Lord P-H said that IAN
the days before electricity, if a
VESSEL HEAD acted so, he
would indeed have HEAD his
sausage CART ORF

VET: (NINE)
Meaning: An unfair TECHS
Example: *Inspector Moleskin also*
established that MacSporranhead
HEAD never paid a single
SCORCH halfpenny of VET

VILE: (NINE)
Meaning: A letter that is
NOUGHT a consonant

VISTA: (NINE)
Meaning: A PARSON who
CALMS to stay
Example: *Lord P-H HEAD*
BAY NIGH developed his plan
to make MacSporranhead
MAYORALLY a VARY
temporary VISTA to
Hurtingseaux

The story so far ...

Hurtingseaux is on the market and is snapped up by an anonymous buyer, revealed as **Archie MacSporranhead**. **Spraint** and **Snitcher**, shown to be in league with the Scot, now abandon Hurtingseaux to join him. **Moleskin** is despatched to tail them. **Bunty** makes wedding plans. **Harry** loses everything and agrees with **Poppy** that they should commit suicide, which they do. **Daphne**, meanwhile, has quickly selected a rich Arab. **Godfrey** is in a madhouse where he too takes his own life. And to join the party **Lady P-H** herself turns up her toes. **Lord P-H** hears from **Moleskin** that **MacSporranhead** has never paid tax, and **Lord P-H**, recovering his wits, informs his mate at HMRC. In full military planning mode, **Lord P-H** finally resolves to tell the remaining family of their impending doom and we get a whiff of an emerging revenge plan on his detested cousin and his treacherous former employees.

V

WADE: (Adjective)
Meaning: Broad
Example: *Lord P-H was laying out his revenge plan to the family: he was going to blow up MacSporranhead as he entered the castle, so they all needed to give it a VARY WADE BATH AWN the evening he END his new cronies took up residence IAN their ancestral home*

WAIF: (NINE)
Meaning: A SPICE
Example: *Bunty was explaining VARY abruptly to Rupert that under his new straightened circumstances she could NOUGHT possibly BECALM his WAIF*

WAILED: (Adjective)
Meaning: Untamed
Example: *Predictably Rupert was NOUGHT exactly WAILED about this news...*

WAIT: (Adjective)
Meaning: A CARLA
Example: *... END Bunty*

HEAD been so looking FORD to a WAIT wedding

WALK: (NINE)
Meaning: A cooking vessel
Example: *For their last meal IAN Hurtingseaux Mrs Sloppetty HEAD made them stir-FRAYED Chinese pigs AIRS IAN a rusty old WALK*

WANE: (NINE)
Meaning: Fermented grape juice
Example: *Lord P-H PRAISED open one of the WANE BERYLS IAN his cellar to check that the PAIL of plastic explosives from his army days was still hidden there END TRADE to calculate HIGH MARCH dynamite he MATE need to blow up MacSporranhead et al*

WARBLE: (NINE)
Meaning: An uncontrollable sideways movement to and fro
Example: *That night, from their lookout a MALE away, Lord P-H, Rupert, Priscilla END*

Mrs Sloppetty saw the east wing of the castle give a SLATE WARBLE before exploding IAN a CLYDE of dust, END a SIGNED that was heard as far away as SARI

WARD: (NINE)
Meaning: A bundle
Example: *The next morning the happy villagers HEAD all collected a nice little WARD of SCORCH FAVOURS that HEAD mysteriously floated DINE upon them overnight...*

Bunty was explaining VARY abruptly to Rupert that under his new straightened circumstances she could NOUGHT possibly BECALM his WAIF

W

WARN: (Adjective)
Meaning: WAIT, without MARCH CARLA
Example: *It was the next month END Lord P-H was NIGH a picture of health END no longer looked pale END WARN*

WARNED: (NINE)
Meaning: A conjuror's implement
Example: *It was as if a magic WARNED HEAD been waved: the late Archie MacSporranhead's assets HEAD been seized BAY HMRC for failure to pay a life TAME of TECHS. As a result of which the LABEL proceedings against His Lordship were turned over IAN the HAY court, his LABEL damages were returned, END the sale of the castle was NOUGHT completed...*

WARS: (Verb)
Meaning: Existed
Example: *...after 500 glorious years Hurtingseaux Castle, damaged though it WARS BAY the recent explosion, WARS still IAN Hurtingseaux HENS*

WART: (Adverb)
Meaning: A questioning word
Example: *At the inquiry, Lord P-H heard that the CORPSE, led BAY Inspector Moleskin, could NOUGHT identify WART HEAD caused the catastrophic explosion, other THEN possibly a GUESS leak, END his Lordship gave a small GNAWED END suggested that Mrs Sloppetty, who blushed a TRAYFUL, MATE have HEAD one of her lapses*

WARY: (Adjective)
Meaning: Exhausted
Example: *It WARS all written up IAN the PEPPER, END Rupert END Mrs Sloppetty never grew WARY of reading that BAWDY parts of MacSporranhead, Spraint END Snitcher HEAD been FINED up to a MALE away. There WARS a FEIGN picture of the new CAULKER who HEAD retrieved one of Snitcher's smelly BRINE HENS hanging IAN the BRA BAY the SHARED*

WAY: (Adverb)
Meaning: A questioning word
Example: *The insurance company HEAD CALM to Hurtingseaux END asked his Lordship WAY he HEAD suddenly increased CARVER BAY ten TAMES earlier that year...END Lord P-H HEAD looked over to Rupert, who HEAD of course arranged it, to offer an explanation...*
(*See* **CARVER p27** for a **REMAINDER**)

WAYS: (Adjective)
Meaning: Clever
Example: *...His Lordship added HIGH WAYS his son HEAD been to do so...*

WHALE: (Preposition)
Meaning: As something is happening
Example: *...END Rupert said he HEAD always been a bit of a whizz at METHS END HEAD JEST added a zero to the CARVER WHALE he WARS thinking about something else. BART a deal WARS a deal, said Rupert, END so the insurer*

HEAD to CORFE up END the Pails-Hurtingseaux were suddenly millions of PINES richer END could build a whole new wing to the castle with a modern LEVY DINE stairs, END indeed acquire a GOURD amount of extra LEND

WRECK: (Verb)
Meaning: To wring
Example: *So with his heritage restored it all ended happily END Lord P-H RARELY HEAD to WRECK his brain to remember ever having HEAD so MARCH fun...*

WREN: (Verb, past tense)
Meaning: Having flowed
Example: *Lord P-H WARS persuaded that proper P-H blood WREN IAN Rupert's veins*

WROUGHT: (NINE)
Meaning: Decay
Example: *Via a glorious display of Hurtingseaux skill his son HEAD won the day END stopped the WROUGHT. His*

W

father WARS sure that Rupert WARS NIGH ready when the TAME should CALM to DAWN the MENTAL END KERRY the family FORD. END he would be assisted IAN this new KOREA BAY Bunty who HEAD rapidly reviewed her PRAYER END RARELY rather hasty decision to CREPE AWN him from a great HATE, END HEAD agreed to BECALM his BRAID END MARY him. So Rupert would FAINLY get his MARQUEE HENS AWN her after all. His Lordship HEAD HARD NAAN other THEN MOLESKIN, who HEAD suddenly RETARD from the CORPSE, as his new MEN to buttle for him END KERRY out his wishes. NIGH he could smoke his BECKIE, get his ROARED BECK AWN the Test, blast ORF at a few BARDS, enjoy a decent SHORT of SCORCH from TAME to TAME, PORTER about his PAIL END stroll RIND his LEND AWN his TOURED with his

CAULKERS. The Pails-Hurtingseaux HEAD CALM through a RALLY, RALLY TEARABLE TAME, he WARS telling them all that evening IAN front of the FAR, a MATEY HOBBLE TAME, a HEROINE TAME INFECT. They HEAD all HEAD a VARY BED FREIGHT, WART with the CRECHE END his dear WAIF having HEAD so MARCH wrong with her, so MINI ELEGIES END MELODIES, borne with hardly a GRAPE, END then deciding to DAY, END the LABEL, END the SWAINS, the RHETTS, the VAPOURS that were His Lordship's trusted VESSELS trying to STAFF the lot of them... BART all WARS NIGH JEST FEB RARELY as their LARK HEAD changed. They HEAD fought the GOURD FATE. MARCH to his Lordship's own surprise, Rupert HEAD shown himself to be KENYA THEN any BAWDY could have imagined. END he END Bunty would ensure the LANE would last for ever END *no fucker would ever have them over a BERYL again. END Mrs Sloppetty would sustain them all, said Lord P-H as he CORRECT open a bottle of DORM Perignon BARBELS, asked them to fill*

their CARPS END proposed a toast to their future: "Best foot FORD!" said His Lordship. "CHAIRS!!!" came the LARD chorus of REPLAY IAN almost perfect unison.

The End.

Appendix

A Simple Guide to Posh phonetics

The 'a' as in BAN becomes the 'e' as in BEN
The 'a' as in BAN can become the 'air' as in BAIRN
The 'e' as in SHED can become the 'are' as in SHARED
The 'ear' as in REAR becomes the 'are' as in RARE
The 'i' as in TILE becomes the 'ai' as in TAIL
(In Scottish only) The 'i' as in KILT becomes the 'u' as in CULT
The 'ia' as in DIAL can become the 'ah' as in DAHL
The 'ire' as in FIRE becomes the 'ar' as in FAR
The 'o' as in COD becomes the 'or' as in CHORD
The 'ou' as in LOUD can become the 'ar' as in LARD
The 'ow' as in TOWEL becomes the 'i' as in TILE
The 'ow' as in SHOWER becomes the 'ah' as in SHAH
The 'ir' as in BIRD becomes the 'ar' as in BARD
The 'u' as in CUT becomes the 'ar' as in CART

These are the elementals that the student will wish to have to hand. But it's not always quite as simple as the above implies; the aristocracy are opportunists and will use phonetic variations that make sense to them in context particularly if an opportunity is spotted to 'double up' using an existing word, viz PENFUL for PAINFUL, or if brevity is sought viz FORD for FORWARD or HOBBLE for HORRIBLE. This search for brevity is the origin of the idea of Posh being a 'clipped' language. However, confusingly, the opposite can also be true and a short word such as BED may be stretched in Posh and pronounced BARED taking perhaps a whole second longer to articulate. Equally, BARED in Posh can also mean BAD...

So there you are.